W9-DHY-482

The Basic Essentials of KNOTS FOR THE OUTDOORS

by Cliff Jacobson

Illustrations by
Cliff Moen

ICS BOOKS, INC.
Merrillville, Indiana

THE BASIC ESSENTIALS OF KNOTS FOR THE OUTDOORS

10 9

1st Printing 5-90, 2nd Printing 7-91, 3rd Printing 9-92, 4th Printing 4-93, 5th Printing 3-94, 6th Printing 2-95, 7th Printing 1-96, 8th Printing 9-97

Printed in U.S.A.

Published by:

ICS BOOKS, Inc.
1370 E. 86th Place
Merrillville, IN 46410

DEDICATION

To Bob Roman, a gentle, courageous man.

Library of Congress Cataloging-in-Publication Data

Jacobson, Cliff.
Knots for the outdoors : the basic essentials of / by Cliff Jacobson ; illustrations by Cliff Moen.
p. cm. -- (The Basic essentials series)
ISBN 0-934802-57-2
1. Knots and splices. 2. Outdoor life. I. Title.
VM533.J33 1990
623.88'82--dc20 89-26850
CIP

TABLE OF CONTENTS

FOREWORD

THE BASIC ESSENTIALS OF KNOTS FOR THE OUTDOORS, was conceived from a criticism of my book, CANOEING WILD RIVERS. The letter was from a man who said he'd studied the chapter on knots and hitches, but couldn't get the hang of my diagrams. Fortunately, a friend — who happened to be left-handed — defended the chapter, saying the illustrations were the easiest to follow of any he'd seen.

Suddenly, a revelation: all the knots and hitches in the first edition of CANOEING WILD RIVERS were drawn with my southpaw bias. No wonder the reader had difficulty understanding them!

Needless to say, I had the illustrations re-drawn for "righties" in the second edition, but vowed that in future books, lefties would have an equal share of the action. Included in this book is the left-hand mirror image of every right-handed knot and hitch!

Then, came the matter of *which* knots and hitches to include. One book I checked boasted 65 knots; another had over 300! One popular knot card (whose illustrations weren't simple at all) showed 40 — far more than anyone could need. Truth is, a half dozen well-chosen knots will accomplish most any task, though a meticulous sailor may need (want) twice that many. For my own purposes, as an avid wilderness canoeist and backwoodsman, ten knots/hitches are enough. These, I've starred in the text, and they're the ones you'll want to master. Most of the others are variations of the important ten with very specific recreation outdoor applications and should be learned on a "need to know" basis.

I've purposely deleted all the low utility cutesy knots and hitches. Ditto for most single-purpose mountaineering and sailing knots. The special knots you need to know for these sports are a main-frame chapter in every climbing and sailing text. The 30 knots, plus the most essential splices and lashings, included here, should answer all your needs. Interspersed throughout the book you'll find subtle humor — hyacinths to combat the frustration of learning — from the magic pen of artist Cliff Moen.

Here's wishing you the right or left knot for every occasion. Enjoy!

1. BACKGROUND

To most people, a rope is a rope, and they make no distinction between natural or synthetic fibers. That's too bad, because certain rope materials and weaves excel in certain applications. Here are some things to consider when choosing ropes:

Flexibility: Flexible ropes accept knots more willingly than stiffer weaves, but when coiled, they are more likely to twist and snag. Choose flexible ropes for tying gear on cars, for general utility, and wherever a proper lashing is needed. Ropes with a stiff "hand" are best for life-guard throwing lines and use around water.

Slipperiness: A slippery rope is always a nuisance. Polyethylene and polypropylene ropes are so slippery that they retain knots only if you "lock" them in place with a whipping or security hitch.

Diameter versus strength: The old rule-of-thumb says that if you double the diameter of a rope, you quadruple its strength. This edge-of-the-ballpark guestimate can be refined with tabular data from the Cordage Institute, 45 North St., Hingham, MA 02043. For comparison: *New* quarter inch three-strand nylon rope yields a tensile strength of 1,490 pounds; half inch nylon rope of similar construction tests at 5,750 pounds.

Safe Working Load: Safety factors and working loads are *not* the same for all types of rope or applications, so it is not possible to accurately define "safe working load." The important thing to remember is that estimated "working loads" like those listed in table 2 are simply *guidelines* to product selection. They naturally assume that ropes are in good condition and are being used in non-critical applications, under normal service conditions. Suggested working loads should *always* be reduced where there is danger to life or property, or when the rope will be exposed to shock or sustained stress.

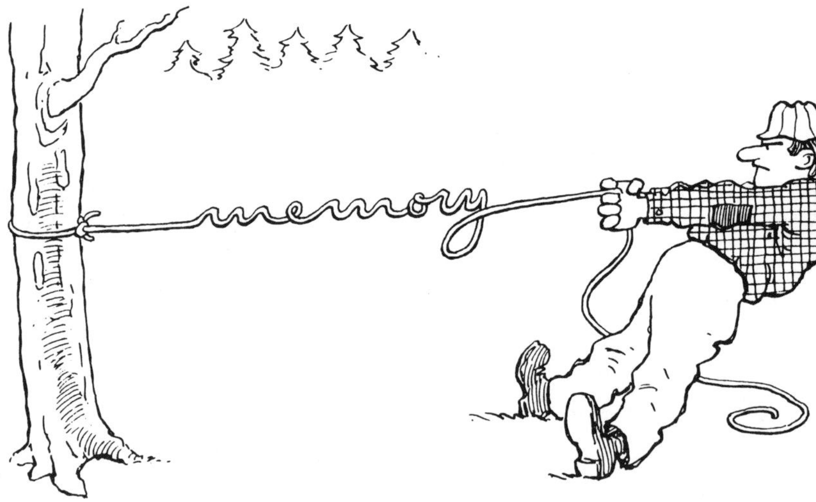

Memory: The ability of a rope to retain a coiled or knotted shape is called "memory." Lariats and throwing lines must necessarily "remember" their manners or they'll snag when played out. Generally, stiffness and good memory go hand-in-hand, but not always. For example, polyethylene line is very flexible but it never forgets its store-bought windings. Most high memory ropes don't take knots very well.

Ultraviolet degradation: Important if your ropes are exposed to sunlight for long periods of time. Table 1 on page 4 provides the comparative specifics.

Stretch: Towing and mountaineering work c
rope: "tie-down" applications require the oppos
ropes (manila/hemp/sisal) shrink when wet, while nylon one
under load. Forty years ago, campers faithfully loosened natural fiber tent guy lines each night before they retired. Today's campers *tighten* nylon ropes when the sun goes down and several times during a storm.

Floatability: Polypropylene and polyethylene (which float) are the logical choice for water ski ropes and throwing lines.

Effects of chemicals: Spill insect repellent on a polypropylene rope and you'll have a handful of mushy fiber. All ropes are affected to some degree by harsh solvents.

Types of Rope

Nylon: Most popular rope fiber, nylon is strong, light, immune to rot, and very shock absorbent. The most popular weaves are *three-strand, twisted*, and *braided* or *sheathed* (figure 1). Twisted rope strands unravel when heated and are therefore difficult to flame-whip when cut. They are best whipped with waxed string, plastic whipping compound, or heat shrunk plastic tubing.

Braided (sheathed) rope is actually two ropes, one inside the other. It's wonderfully pliable and it resists twists and kinks when coiling. Braided rope flame-whips easily and its casing resists abrasion. However, its sheath may mask flaws in the core.

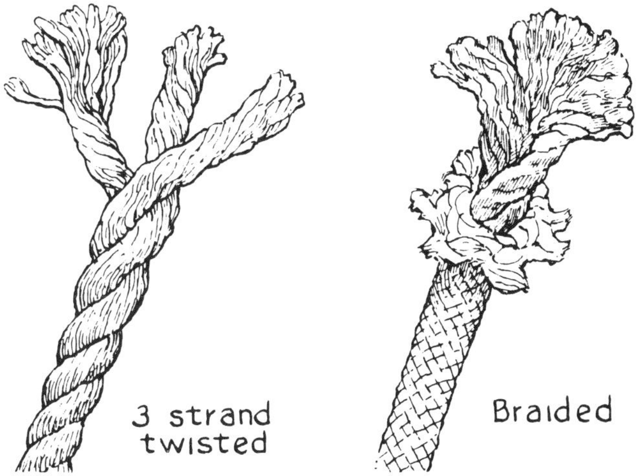

Figure 1

TABLE 1:
COMPARISONS OF SOME COMMON ROPES*

	MANILA	SISAL	COTTON	NYLON	POLYESTER	POLYPRO-PYLENE	POLYETHY-LENE	ARAMID
Strength:								
Breaking tenacity-dry (grams/denier)	5-6.0	4-5.0	2-3.0	7.8-10.4	7.0-9.5	6.5	6.0	18-26.5
Wet strength compared to dry strength	Up to 120%	Up to 120%	Up to 120%	85-90%[1]	100% + [1]	100%	105%	95%
Shock load absorption ability	Poor	Poor	Very Poor	Excellent	Very Good	Very Good	Fair	
Weight:								
Specific gravity	1.38	1.38	1.54	1.14	1.38	.91	.95	1.44
Able to float	No	No	No	No	No	Yes	Yes	No
Elongation:								
Percent at break	10-12%	10-12%	5-12%	15-28%	12-15%	18-22%	20-24%	1.5-3.6%
Creep (extension under sustained load)	Very Low	Very Low		Moderate	Low	High	High	Very low
Effects of Moisture:								
Water absorption of individual fibers	Up to 100%	Up to 100%	Up to 100%	2.0-8.0%	‹1.0%	None	None	3.5-7.0%
Resistance to rot, mildew and deterioration due to marine organisms	Poor	Very Poor	Very Poor	Excellent	Excellent	Excellent	Excellent	Excellent
Degradation:								
Resistance to U.V. in sunlight	Good	Good	Good	Good	Excellent	Fair Black is best	Fair Black is best	Fair[3]
Resistance to aging for properly stored rope	Good	Good	Good	Excellent	Excellent	Excellent	Excellent	Excellent
Rope Abrasion Resistance:								
Surface	Good	Fair	Poor	Very Good	Best	Good	Fair	Fair[3]
Internal	Good	Good	Good	Excellent	Best	Good	Good	Good
Thermal Properties:								
High temperature working limit	300°F	300°F	300°F	250°F	275°F	200°F	150°F	350°F
Low temperature working limit	-100°F	-100°F	-100°F	-70°F	-70°F	-20°F	-100°F	-100°F
Melts at			Chars 300°F	420-480°F	490-500°F	330°F	285°F	800°F Begins to decompose

Chemical Resistance:								
Effect of acids	Will disintegrate in hot diluted & cold concentrated acids	Same as Manila	Same as Manila	Decomposed by strong mineral acids; resistant to weak acids	Resistant to most mineral acids; disintegrate by 95% sulphuric acid	very resistant	Very resistant	Resistant to most weak acids. Strong acids will attack, particularly at high temp. or concentrations.
Effect of alkalis	Poor resistance; will lose strength where exposed	Same as Manila	May swell but will not be damaged	Little or none	No effect cold; slowly disintegrate by strong alkalis at the boil	Very resistant	Very resistant	Resistant to most weak alkalis. Strong alkalis will attack, particularly at high temperatures or concentrations.
Effect of organic solvents	Fair resistance for fiber, but hydrocarbons will remove protective lubricants on rope	Good resistance	Poor resistance	Resistant, soluble in some phenolic compounds and in 90% formic acid	Generally unaffected; soluble in some phenolic compounds	Soluble in chlorinated hydrocarbons at 160°F	Same as polypropylene	Resistant to most ketones, alcohols, oils, hydrocarbons.

[1]Grades with special overfinishes are available to enhance wet strength properties. [2]Based on DuPont Kevlar® data. [3]Excellent when jacketed.

*I am indebted to the Cordage Institute, 42 North St., Hingham, MA 02043, for use of these specifications.

Polyethylene: Inexpensive, slippery, slightly elastic, unaffected by water, available in colors, and it floats — popular for towing water skiers.

Polypropylene: Similar to polyethylene but less slippery and more elastic (a better rope).

Polyester (Dacron TM) is *the* material for sailboat sheet and mooring lines and every place you need a rope that is dimensionally stable and resistant to ultraviolet light.

TABLE 2:
STRENGTH IN POUNDS FOR SOME THREE-EIGHTHS INCH DIAMETER STANDARD CONSTRUCTION THREE-STRAND TWISTED AND EIGHT-STRAND PLAITED ROPES**

	TENSILE STRENGTH	WORKING LOAD
Manila	1220	122
Sisal	1080	108
Nylon	3340	278
Polyester	3340	334
Polypropylene	2440	244
Polyester/polypropylene composite	2430	243
Kevlar (Aramid by Dupont, Inc.):		
wire rope construction		3,000

***Working Loads* are for rope in good condition, in non- critical applications, and under normal service conditions. These are guidelines only.

Natural fiber ropes: Except for cotton, which is still used for sash cords and clothes line, natural fiber ropes like manila, sisal, hemp, and jute, have almost gone the way of the passenger pigeon. Natural fibers have a nice hand; they coil well and hold knots tenaciously. But they rot easily and for their weight, aren't very strong. For example, the tensile strength in pounds of new manila rope is roughly 8,000 times the square of its diameter in inches.

Thus, new three-eighths inch manila will theoretically hold about .375 x .375 x 8,000 = 1125 pounds (the Cordage Institute figure is 1220) — hardly a match for the modern synthetics in table 2.

Kevlar (TM) is a gold-colored synthetic fiber developed by the Dupont Co. It's used as a tire cord fiber for bullet-resistant vests and as fabrication material for ultra-light canoes and kayaks. Kevlar rope is very light (specific gravity is 1.44); it's about four times as strong as steel of the same diameter, and so expensive that it is recommended only for applications where extreme strength, light weight, low elongation and non-corrosion are major concerns. Kevlar is difficult to cut, even with the sharpest tools.

A SPARE 50 FOOT HANK OF NYLON CAN BE USEFUL FOR RIGGING A RAIN TARP IN A STORM

Preparing A New Rope

I wouldn't think of striking off into the backcountry without one or two 50 foot hanks of 5/16" twisted nylon rope. On occasion, my ropes have served to extract a rock-pinned canoe from a raging rapid; to rig a nylon rain tarp in the teeth of a storm; as a strong clothesline and swimmer's rescue rope; to secure gear on my truck ... and once, to haul my old Volkswagen beetle out of a knee-deep ditch.

A well-maintained rope may last a decade. An ill-kept one won't survive a season. First order of business is to seal the ends (called "whipping") by one of these methods, so they won't unravel.

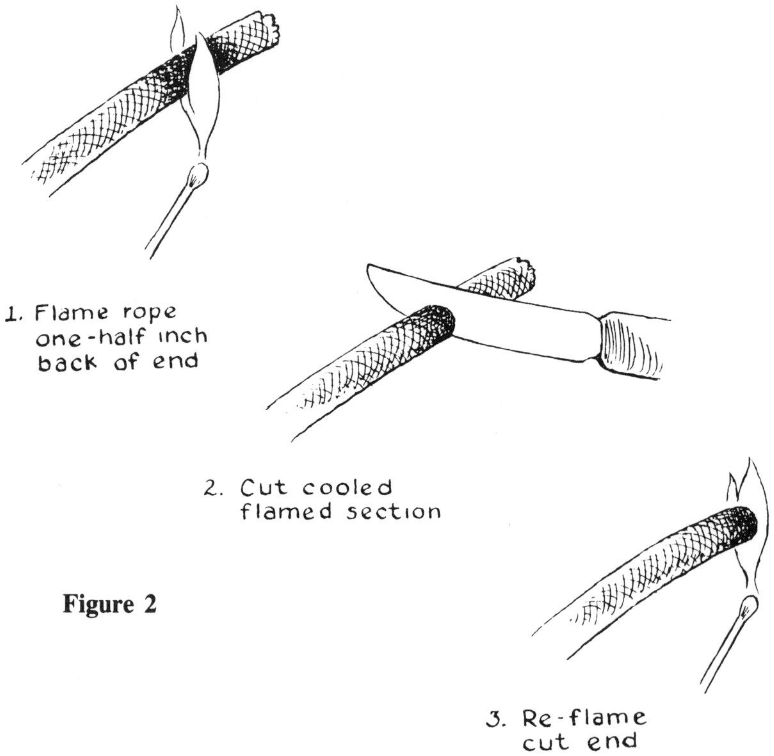
1. Flame rope
one-half inch
back of end
2. Cut cooled
flamed section
3. Re-flame
cut end

Figure 2

Flame-whipping: Most synthetic ropes flame-whip easily. All you need is a cigarette lighter or a small propane blow- torch. Braided (sheathed) ropes, including parachute cord, should be seared full circle, just back of the ends, then cut square through the (cooled) flamed section with a sharp blade. For a neat, trim look, finish by lightly flaming the cut end, as illustrated in figure 2. This two-step procedure will prevent the ends from cauliflowering when heat is applied.

Figure 3

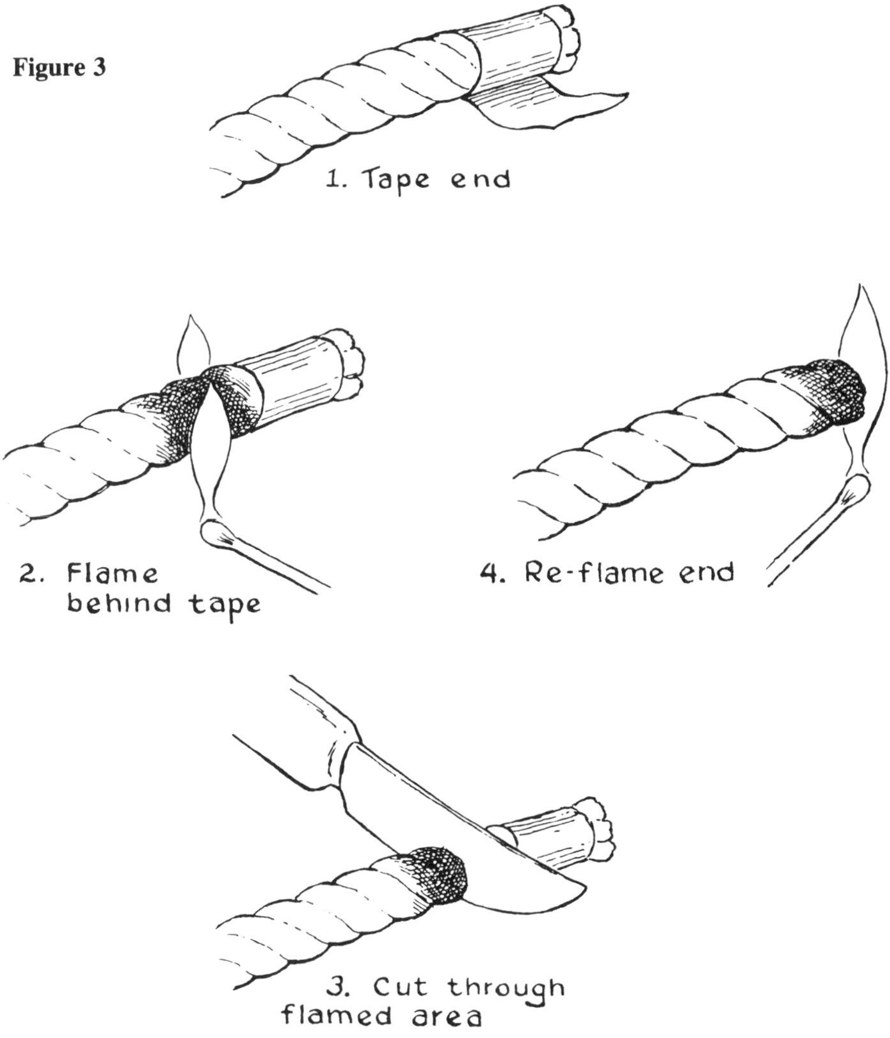
1. Tape end
2. Flame behind tape
4. Re-flame end
3. Cut through flamed area

Twisted rope tends to unravel when flame is applied. The solution is to wrap the end firmly with tape, then sear the area behind the tape, all around. When the rope has cooled, remove the tape, cut the end square through the singed section, and re-flame the end as illustrated in figure 3. The length of your whipping should equal the diameter of the rope.

Figure 4

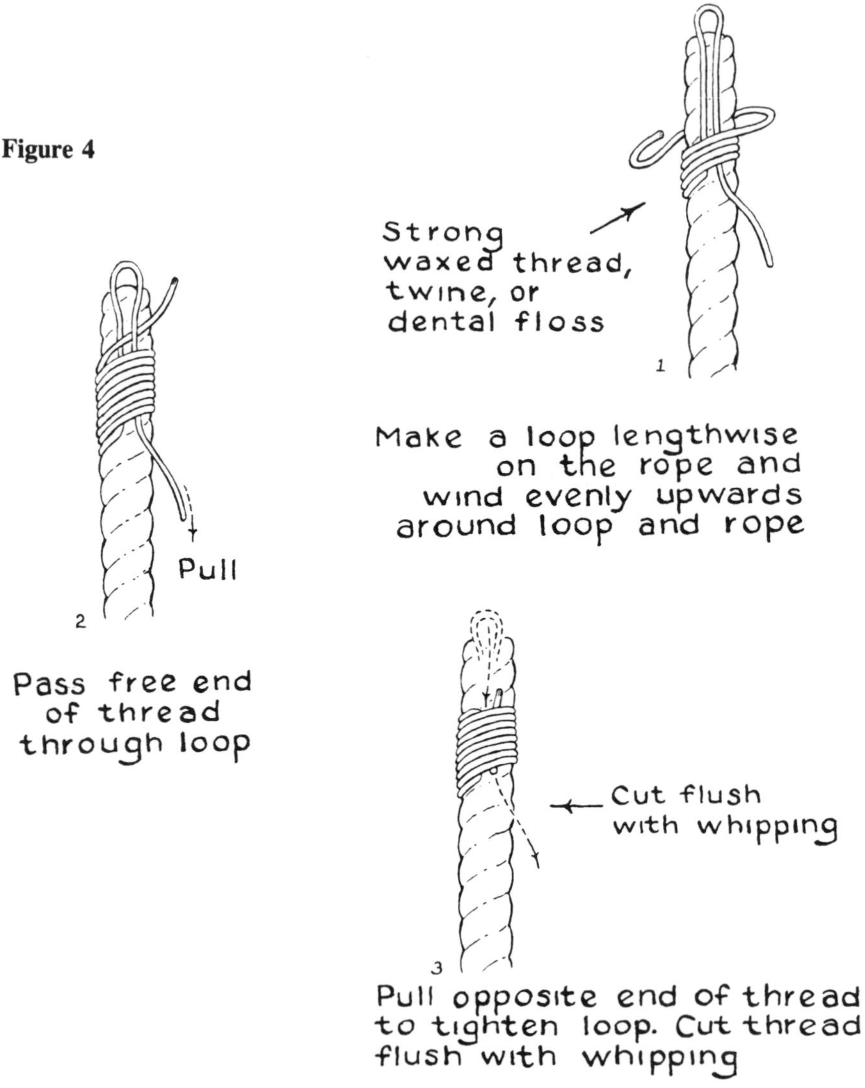

Strong waxed thread, twine, or dental floss
1
Make a loop lengthwise on the rope and wind evenly upwards around loop and rope
Pull
2
Pass free end of thread through loop
Cut flush with whipping
3
Pull opposite end of thread to tighten loop. Cut thread flush with whipping

String whipping: Time-consuming to do but more reliable than flame or liquid plastic. The "simple whip" illustrated above (figure 4) is adequate for most chores. For best results, use shoemaker's waxed thread or heavy button/carpet thread (dental floss works great) and wind *against* the lay of the rope, towards the end.

Plastic-whippings: Dip the rope end into "liquid plastic rope whipping," and allow it to dry. For a neater look, apply heat-shrunk plastic sleeves to the rope ends. These products come in a variety of colors and are available at most marinas.

Coiling Your Rope For Proper Storage

On a canoe trip some years ago, one canoe swamped in a heavy rapid. There was a bouldery falls just downstream so we had to get a throwing line to the men in the water immediately. Two 50 foot nylon ropes, which were properly coiled for throwing, were heaved to the pair who were hanging on to the gunnels of the water-filled canoe. The men caught the ropes and were rescued just 50 feet above the falls!

Here's how to keep your ropes coiled and ready for use:

Old Navy Method: Figure 5

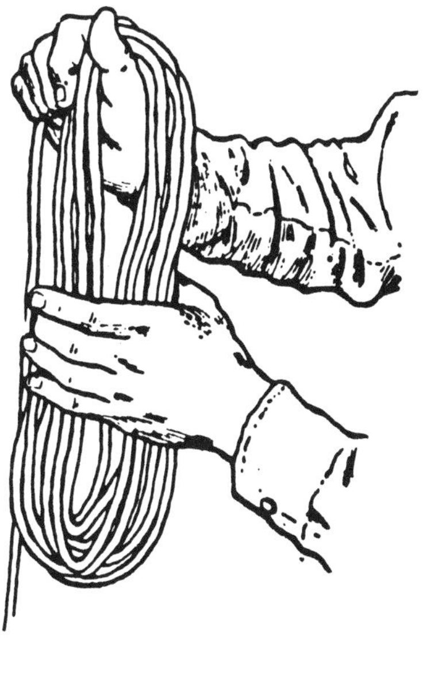

Step 1.

1. Coil the rope: take care to lay each coil carefully into place, twisting it a half turn so it will lay without twisting. Then, grasp the main body of the rope with one hand and place your thumb through the eye of the coils to hold them in place as shown in Figure 5, step 1.

Step 2.

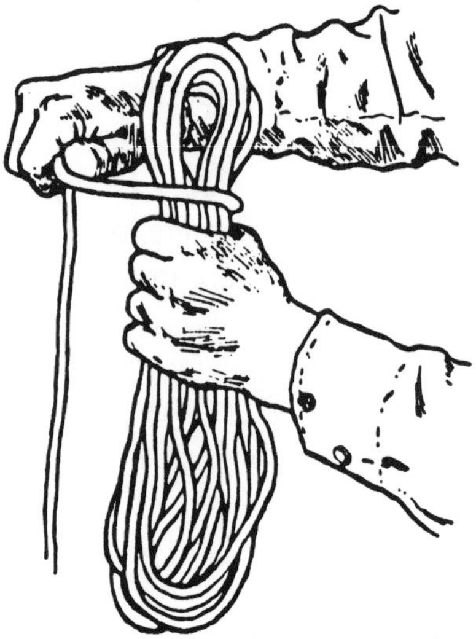

2. Remove the last two coils of rope; take this long free end, and wind it around the main body of the rope several times (figure 5, step 2). Wind the free end *downward*, toward the hand holding the rope body. Wind evenly and snugly. Don't make the coils too tight.

Step 3.

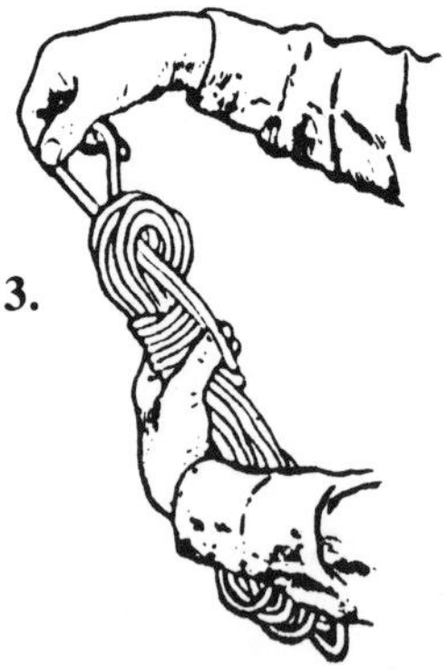

Step 4.

3. Form a loop with the free end of the rope as shown in step 3, and push it through the eye of the rope body.

4. Grasp the wound coils with one hand and the rope body with the other hand and slide the coils upward tightly against the loop. The rope is now coiled and secured (step 4). Pulling the free end of the rope will release the line, which can quickly be made ready for throwing.

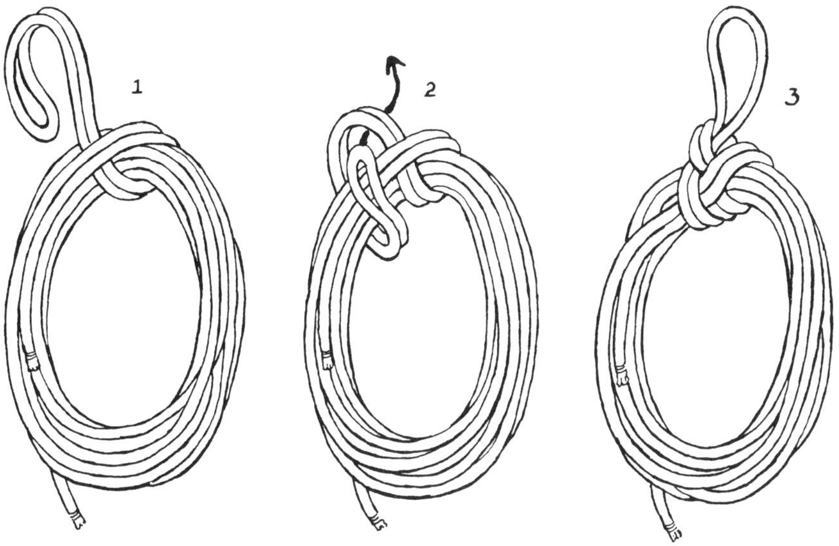

Sailors' Stowing Coil: Figure 6

This method doesn't look as neat, but it better preserves the integrity of the coils (they're less likely to snag when the rope is tossed out):

Procedure: Coil the rope and double the last few feet to form a long loop. Wind the loop around the coil and secure with a pair of half hitches as illustrated. Hang your rope from the loop at top.

How To Care For Your New Rope

Abrasion is the kiss-of-death, so keep your ropes clean. I wash mine once-a-year in a sudsy tub of liquid detergent. Then, I coil and air-dry my ropes and store them in a cool, dry place.

Tip: To remove the "memory" of store-bought coils, slightly stretch a new rope (tie it off tight between two trees) for an hour or two. An old snagged rope may forget its windings if you soak it briefly in water then administer the stretch treatment.

All ropes — natural and synthetic — are injured to some extent by ultraviolet light. So keep your ropes out of the sun as much as possible.

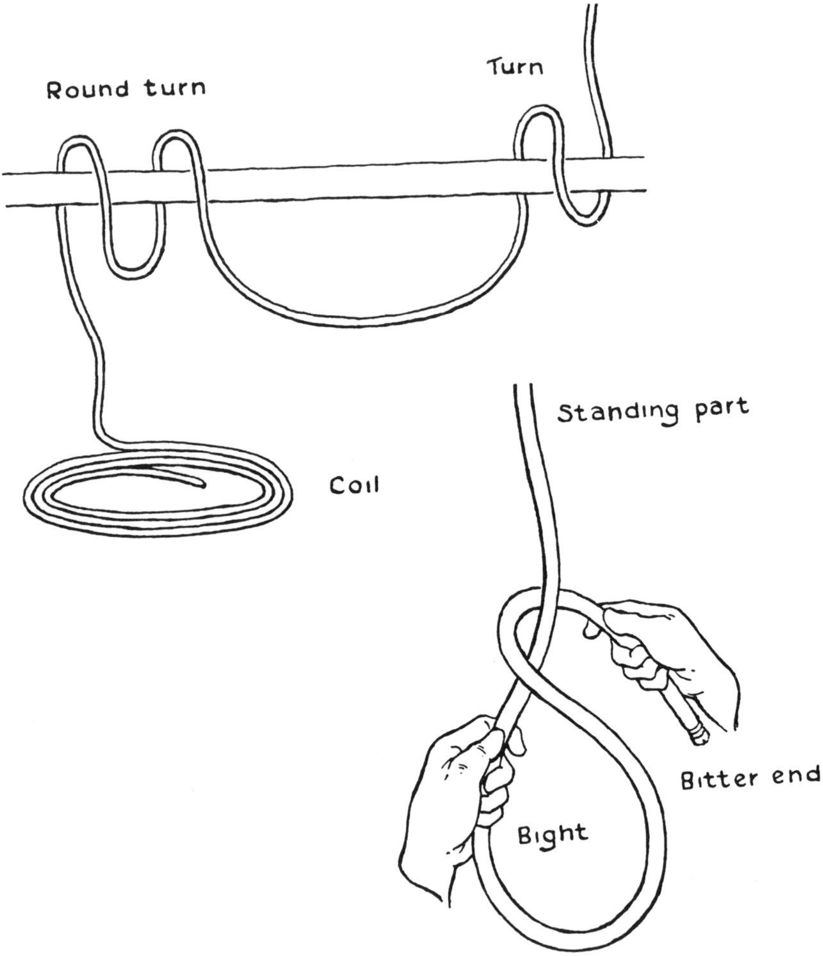

Rope Nomenclature: Figure 7

All the knots and hitches in this book may be mastered by simply following the diagram(s) and reading the accompanying text. You don't need to know any of these "rope terms" to understand the illustrations or descriptions. Nonetheless, no knot book would be complete without the basic nomenclature, which you may commit to memory or disregard, depending on your perspective.

2. KNOTS

Left-handed knots are indicated by the LH symbol and appear on the *left-side* of the text or in a special box adjacent to the right-hand knot versions. To save space, the knots, judged by the author as "universal," are illustrated in right-hand form only.

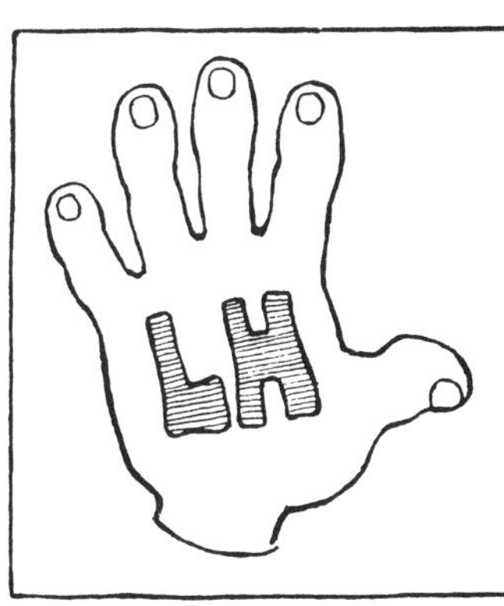

How Strong Are Knots?

As a general rule, knots reduce rope strength by about 50 percent. Table 3 indicates the approximate breaking strength of some popular knots. Note that splices (which really aren't knots at all) detract barely, if at all, from a rope's breaking strength — the reason why they are the preferred way to join lines.

TABLE 3
APPROXIMATE BREAKING STRENGTH IN PERCENT OF SOME COMMON KNOTS*

Anchor (fishermans) bend: 70
Bowline: 60
Bowline on a bight: 60
Carrick bend: 65
Clove hitch: 75
Figure eight (end) knot: 48
Monofilament fishing knot (clinch knot): 80
Single overhand knot (half a "granny"): 45
Pipe hitch: 70
Two half-hitches: 75
Sheepshank: 45
Square (reef) knot: 45
Timber hitch: 70
Eye splice: 95
Short splice: 90

*Figures are derived from: *Plymouth Cordage*, 1946, and from tests by Scovell, Miller, Dent, Trumpler, and Day, as reported in *The Art of Knotting and Splicing*, by Cyrus Lawrence Day, 1970; and *Ropework*, Practical Knots Hitches and Splices, by J. Grant Dent, University of Minnesota Agricultural Extension Service, U.S.D.A. 1964.

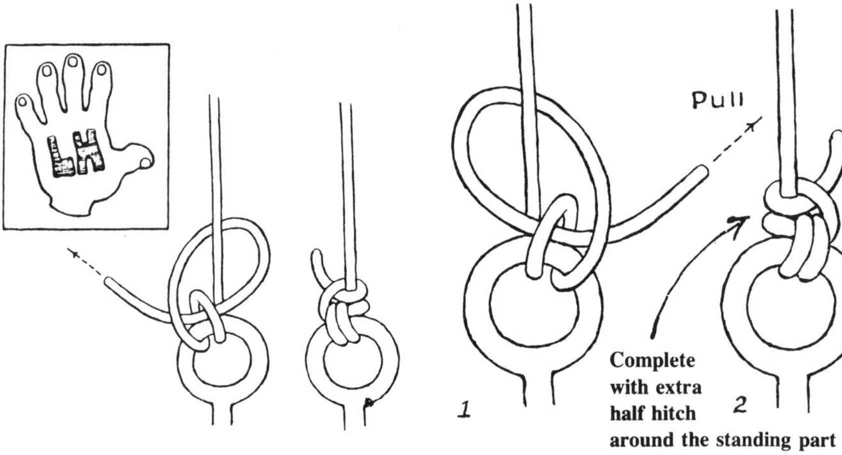

LH
Pull
1
Complete with extra half hitch around the standing part
2

*ANCHOR (FISHERMAN'S) BEND: Figure 2-1

With a breaking strength of approximately 70 percent, the Anchor Bend is one of the strongest knots known. It won't slip or jam and it can be easily untied. The hitch was originally used to tie the anchor ring on sailing vessels — testimony to its reliability. Probably the best hitch to use for mooring small boats, the anchor bend also works great for securing lures to monofilament fishing line. Its one drawback is that it is difficult to make in large diameter rope. Belt-and-suspenders folk sometimes complete the bend with a bowline on the standing part.

*These are the most useful knots — the ones you'll want to master first.

LET'S SEE NOW - THE RABBIT GOES AROUND THE TREE AND BACK DOWN THE HOLE

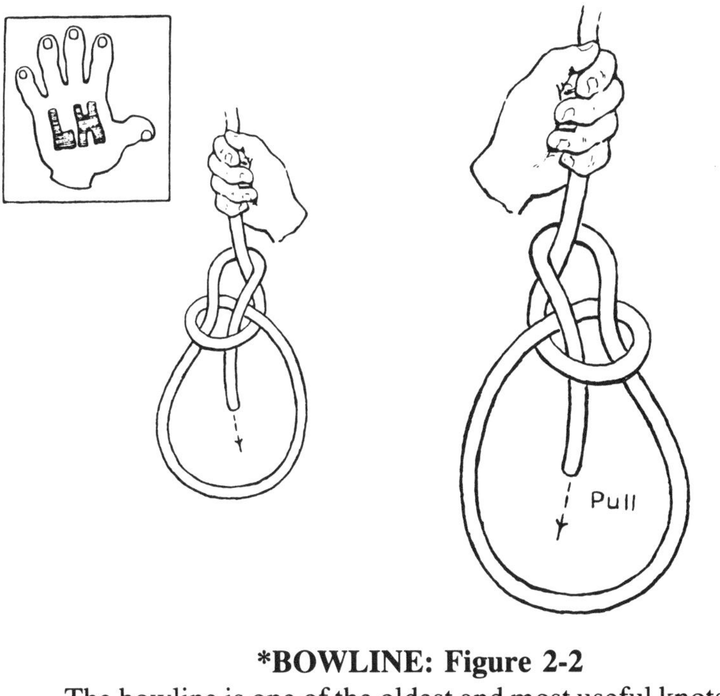

***BOWLINE: Figure 2-2**

The bowline is one of the oldest and most useful knots. Captain John Smith (1627) considered it one of the three most important knots aboard ship — the other two being the sheepshank and the wall knot (a crown-like end knot which is infrequently used today).

The bowline is a very secure knot which won't slip, regardless of the load applied. It is commonly used by mountain climbers to tie their climbing ropes around their waists. Use this knot whenever you want to put a non-slip loop on the end of a line.

Beginners are often told to make the bowline by forming a loop, or "rabbit hole." The rabbit (bitter or free end of the rope) comes up through the hole, around the tree (standing part of the rope) and back down the hole. The bowline will slip a few inches before it tightens, so allow an extra-long free end.

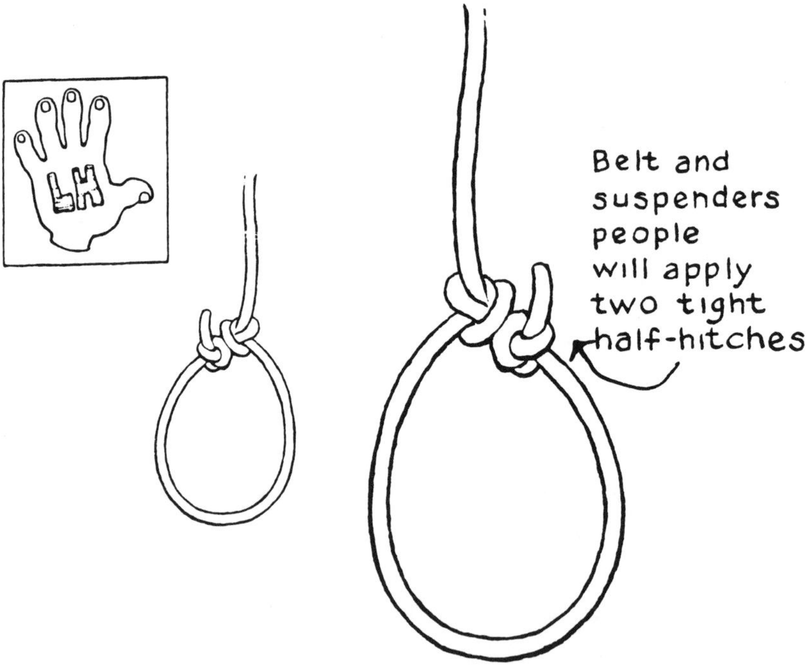
LH
Belt and
suspenders
people
will apply
two tight
half-hitches

LOCKING BOWLINE: Figure 2-3

For complete security, especially in slippery plastic ropes, complete the bowline with two half-hitches, as illustrated. This "improved bowline" is sometimes called the *locking bowline*. Page 30 shows how to tie a basic "half-hitch."

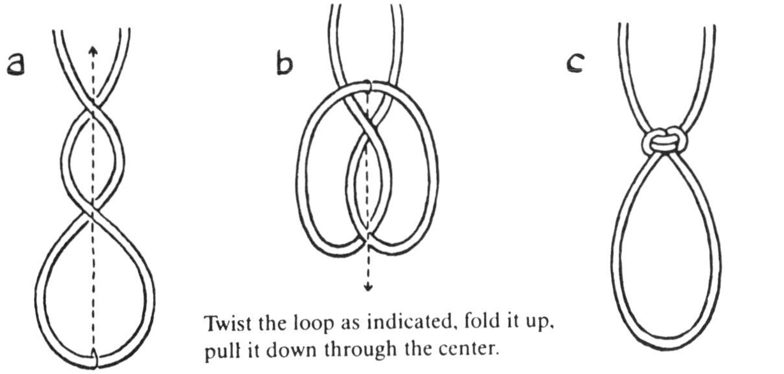

Twist the loop as indicated, fold it up, pull it down through the center.

***BUTTERFLY NOOSE: Figure 2-4 (Right-hand only)**

Mountain climbers use the *butterfly noose* to attach carabiners or whenever they need a non-slip loop in the middle of a rope. Butterfly loops are secure and will accommodate a load in any direction. They can be spaced along a line to provide purchase points for a winch line — essential in canoe rescue work. Need to pull a long rope tight? Evenly spaced "butterfly nooses" will give each person a secure handhold. The knot is also handy for fastening gut leaders to monofilament fishing line.

Like the bowline, the butterfly noose will not jam, regardless of load direction. Also called the "lineman's loop," this knot was once popular with telephone line men.

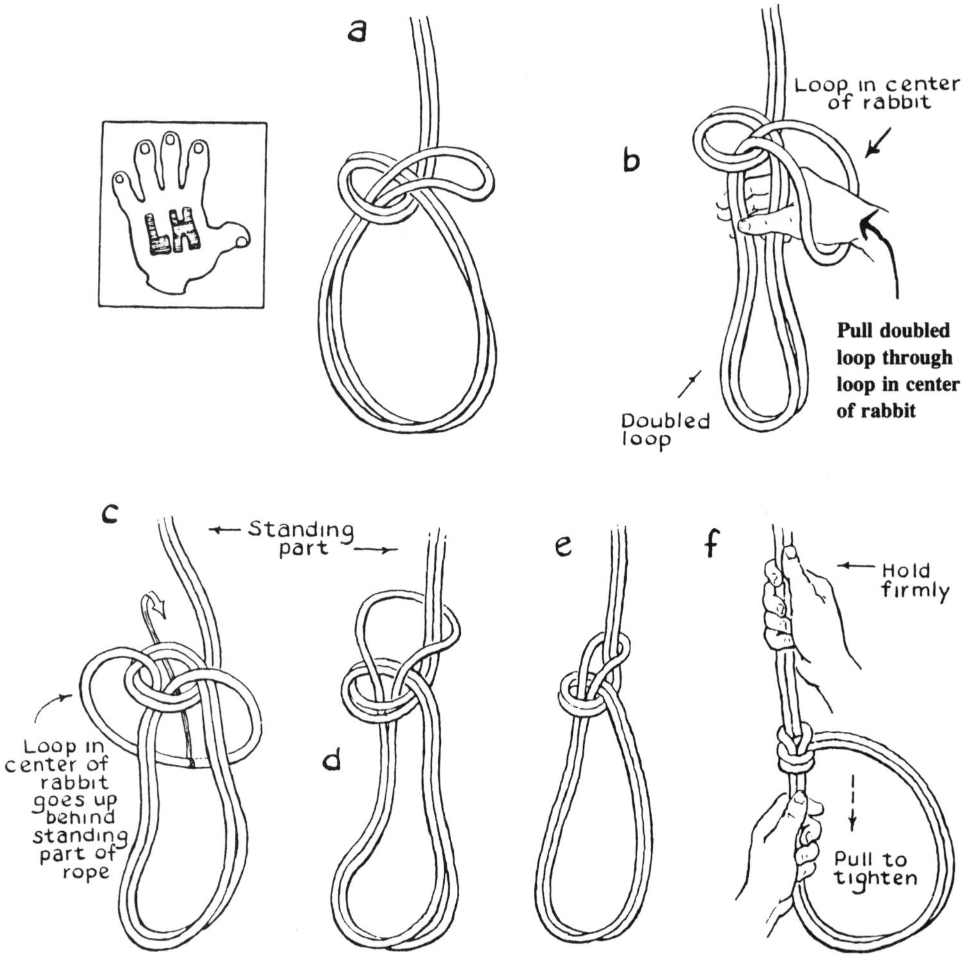

BOWLINE ON A BIGHT: Figure 2-5a-e

Use this whenever you need to make a two-legged "bosun's chair" for rescue work, or when you need a non-slip loop in the middle of a rope when both ends are inaccessible.

The *bowline on a bight* differs from the conventional bowline in that the loop in the center of the "rabbit" (see description of *bowline* on page 17) is passed over the doubled loop which is hanging below then forced up behind the standing part of the rope. Hold the rope firmly with your left hand as you pull down with your right to tighten the knot.

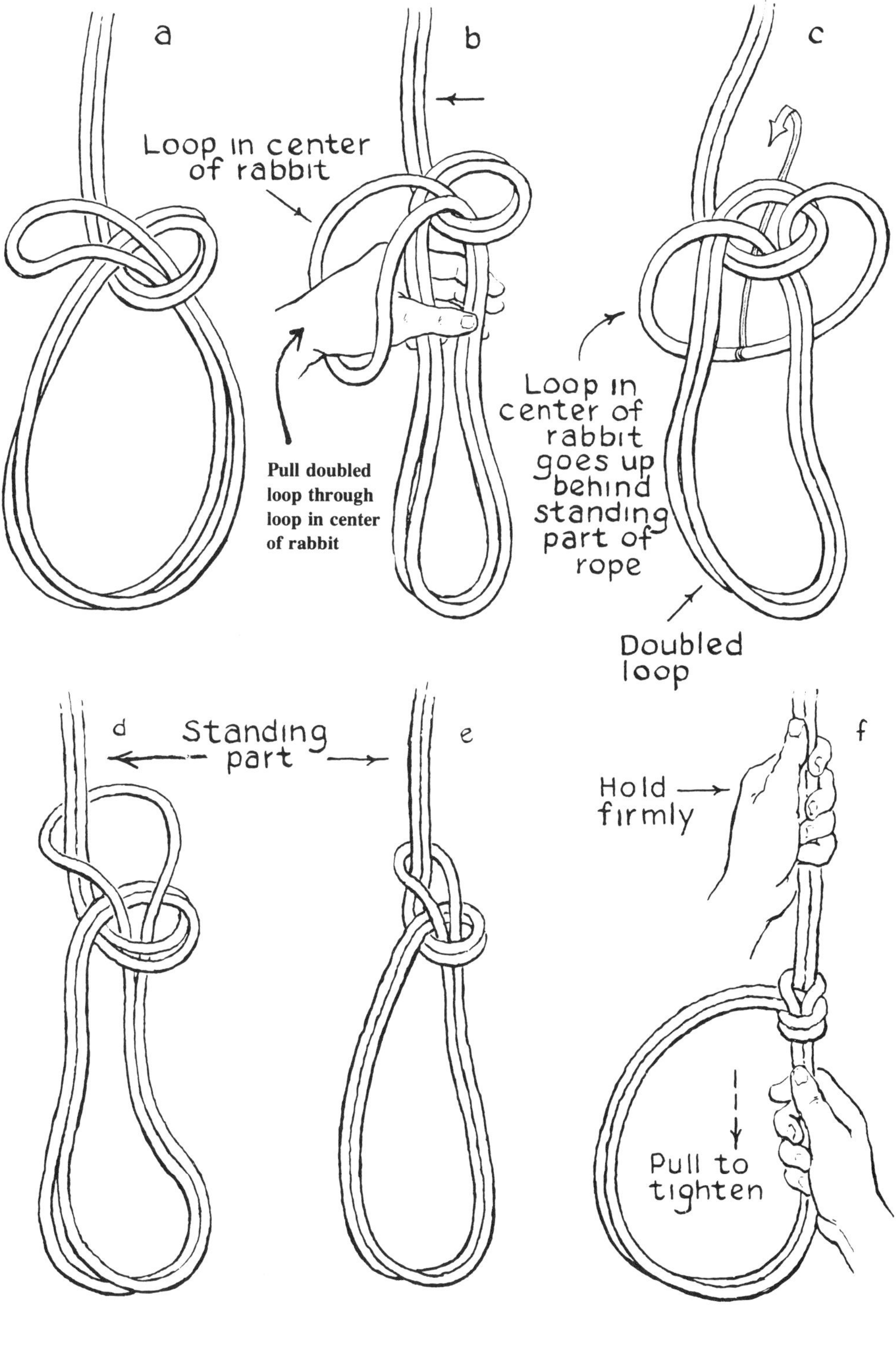
a
b
c
Loop in center of rabbit
Pull doubled loop through loop in center of rabbit
Loop in center of rabbit goes up behind standing part of rope
Doubled loop
d
e
f
Standing part
Hold firmly
Pull to tighten

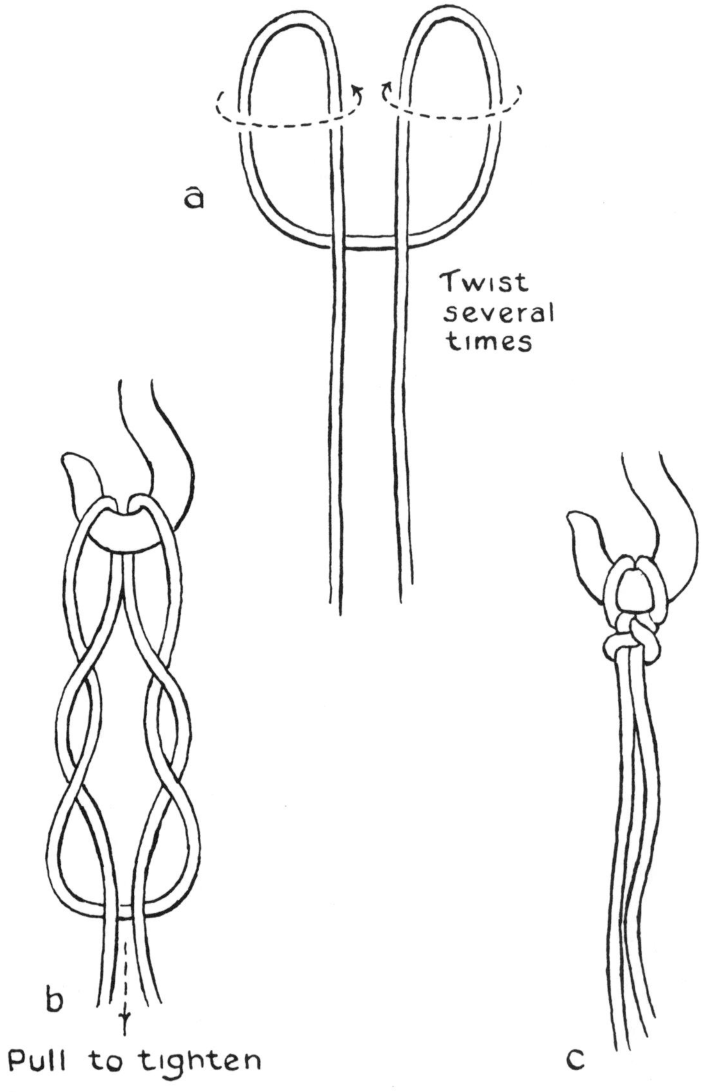
a
Twist several times
b
Pull to tighten
c

CAT'S PAW: Figure 2-6 (Right-hand only)

Here's a slick way to attach a rope to a hook or the towing link of a vehicle. The *cat's paw* is secure under heavy load, yet it comes apart easily — the reason why it remains popular with longshoremen and movers.

Form two loops at the end of your rope, twist them around several times, and hook them in place. That's all there is to it.

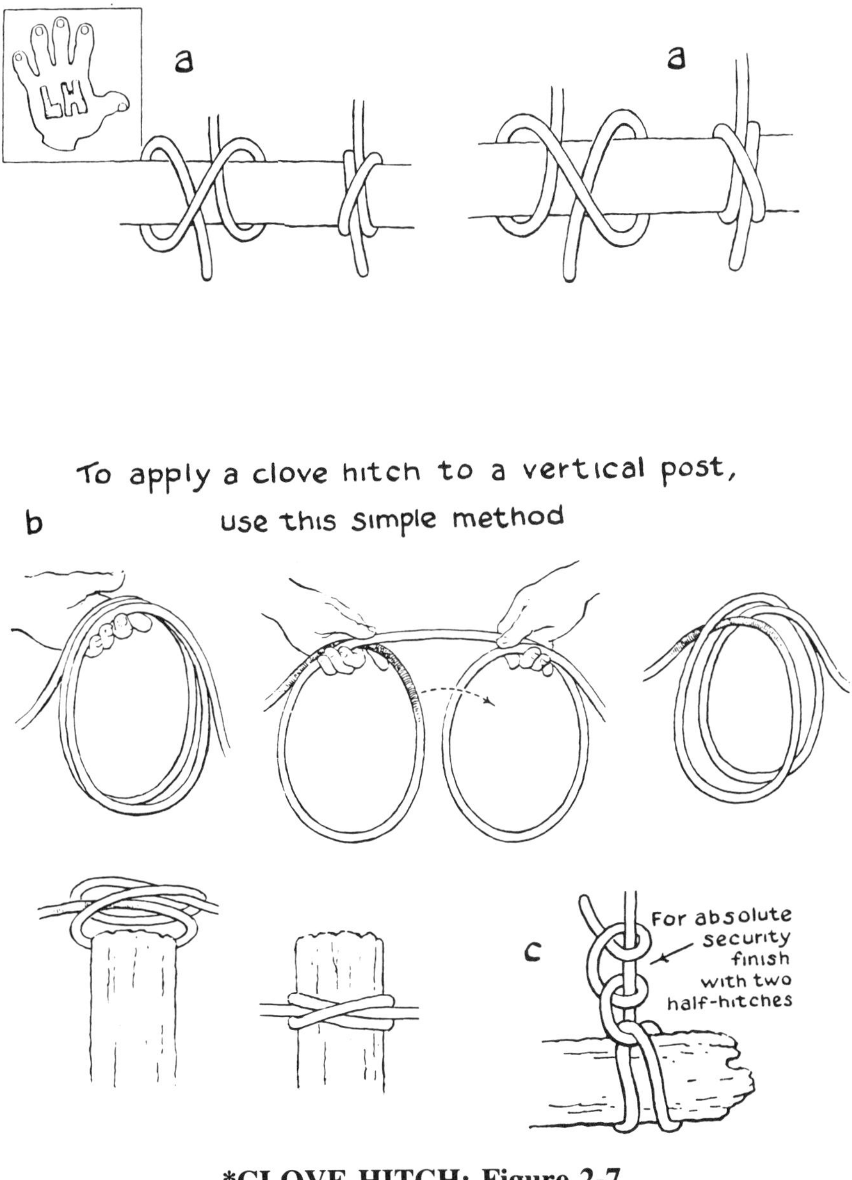
a
a
To apply a clove hitch to a vertical post,
b
use this simple method
c
For absolute security finish with two half-hitches

***CLOVE HITCH: Figure 2-7**

A popular knot for mooring boats to piers and pilings, and to secure ratlines to the shrouds on sailboats, the *clove hitch* is also a common "starter" knot for lashings and the diamond hitch. When absolute security is needed, finish the knot with one or two half-hitches, as illustrated in figure 7c.

1

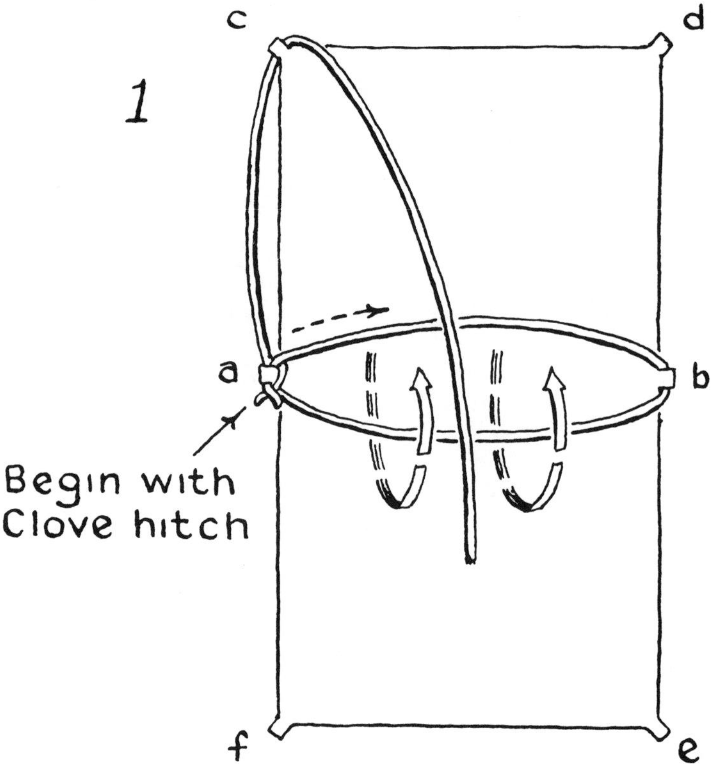

2

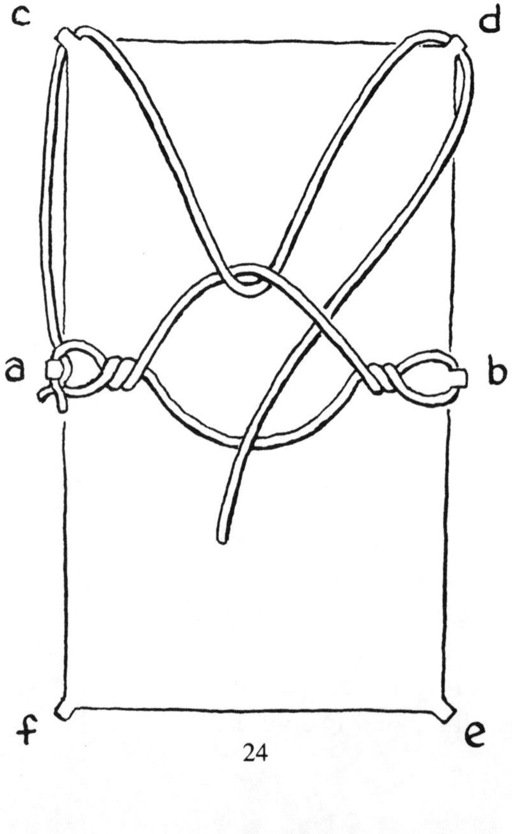

4

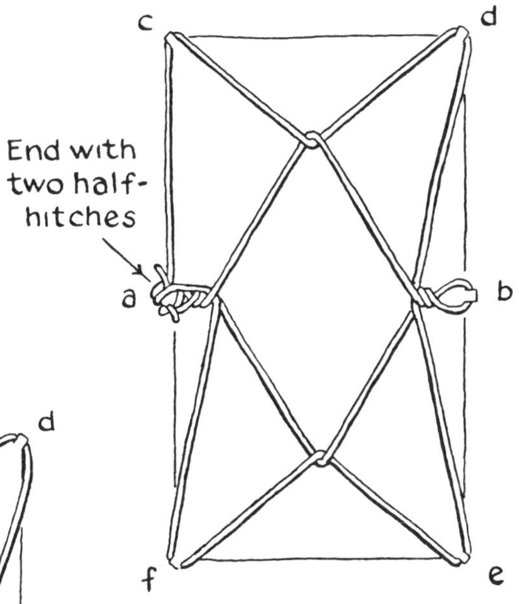

3

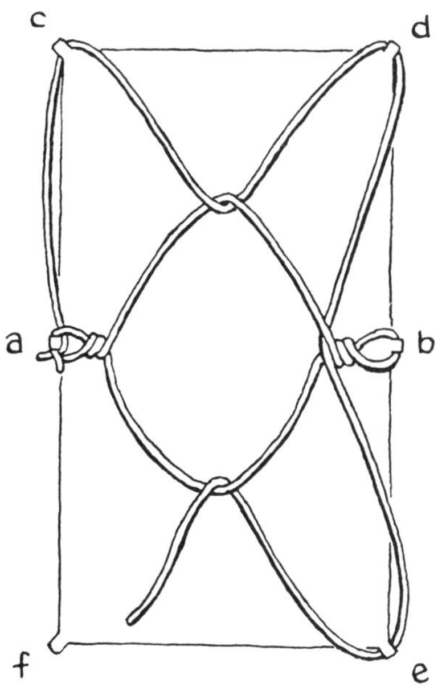

DIAMOND HITCH: Figures 2-8 (Right-hand only)

For centuries, this classic hitch has been used by prospectors, fur traders and trappers to secure gear on pack animals. Use the diamond hitch to tie a load onto a cartop or trailer: all you need is one long rope. The real value of the diamond hitch is that strain on one part of the rope is taken up elsewhere in the hitch, which causes the line to tighten. The "six-point" diamond suspension provides security even when the load shifts.

To apply a diamond hitch to a pack frame, begin by tying a rope end at point "a", using a *clove hitch* (see page 23). Then, loop the line around "b" and "c", as illustrated. Next, twist the horizontal center strands a couple times and feed the bitter (free) end of the rope through, looping it over the frame points in the order illustrated. When the hitch is complete, pull the rope to tighten the hitch, then tie it off where you started it, with two half-hitches.

Note: when tying to a pack animal, the hitch usually originates and ends at the ring in the girth strap, and the "diamond" in the center appears much larger than illustrated.

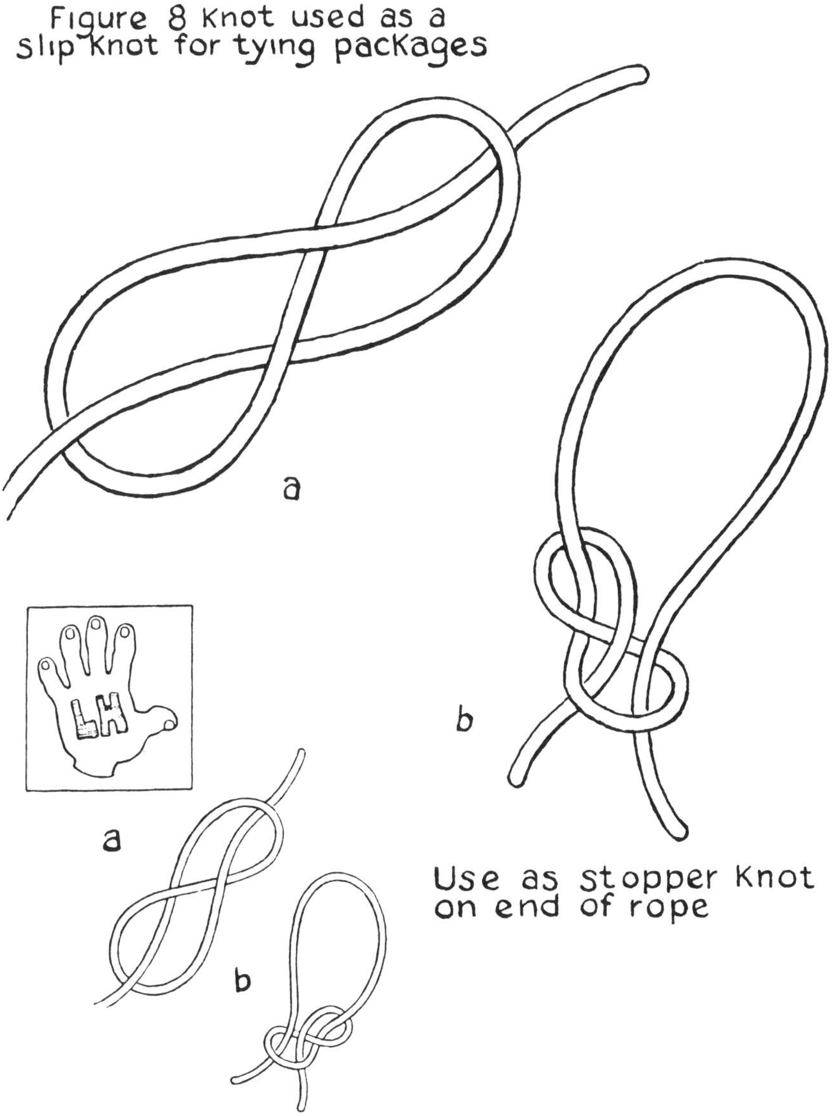
Figure 8 knot used as a slip knot for tying packages
a
b
a
b
Use as stopper knot on end of rope

FIGURE EIGHT (END) KNOT: Figure 2-9a, b

Use this beautifully symmetrical knot as a "stopper" knot on the end of a rope. It functions like an overhand knot, but with more bulk. The knot also makes a convenient slip-noose for tying packages. When used in this manner it is called the "packer's" or "parcel" knot.

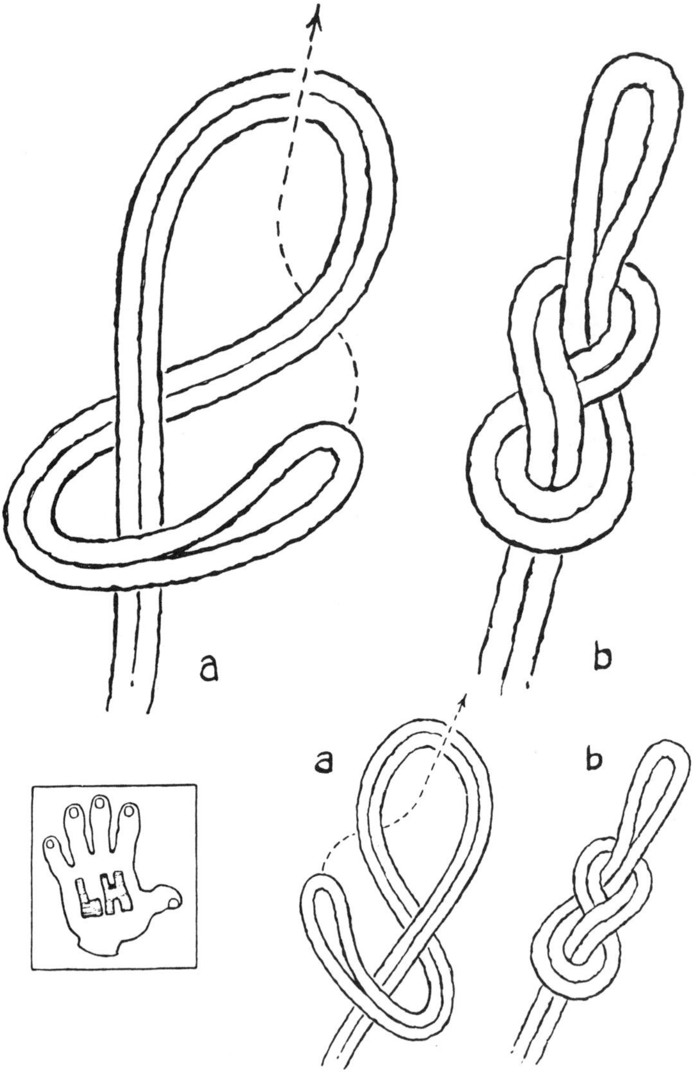

FIGURE 8 LOOP: Figure 2-10

The *figure 8 loop* is a sort of shlocky bowline. It's easy to make and it holds securely, even in slippery, synthetic rope (something which cannot be said of the bowline.) If you need a quick, non-slip loop in the middle of a rope, the *figure 8* is much faster to make than a *bowline on a bight*. It's also ideal for putting a loop on hard-to-grasp twine and thread. However, the knot jams under load, so forget about untying it later. Use the *figure 8 loop* for thin cordage; stick with the bowline for rope.

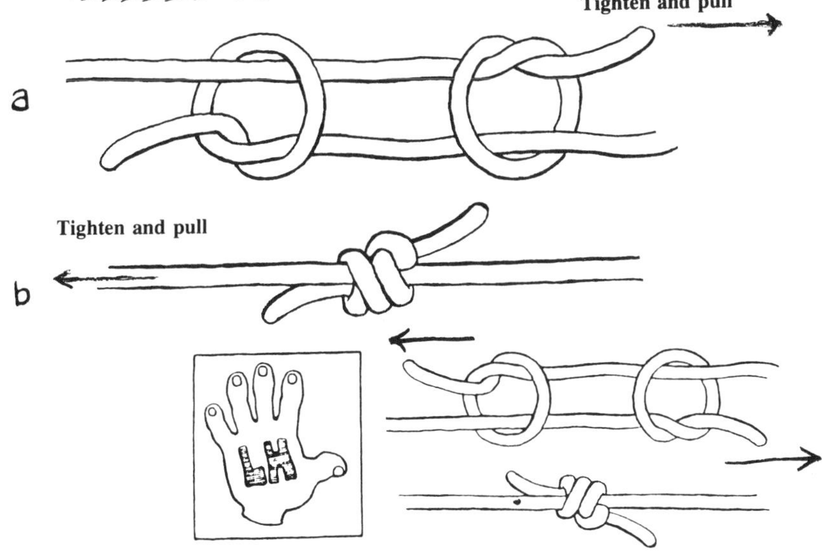

FISHERMAN'S KNOT (WATER KNOT): Figure 2-11

Once popular for tying leader to line, the *fisherman's knot* is now seldom used for this purpose as there are better knots for slippery nylon. However, mountaineers like it for tying ropes together because the knot has a finished, symmetrical look. Canoeists and kayakers use the *fisherman's knot* to secure rope "grab loops" to the ends of their boats. Note: the knot is somewhat stronger when tied *against* the lay.

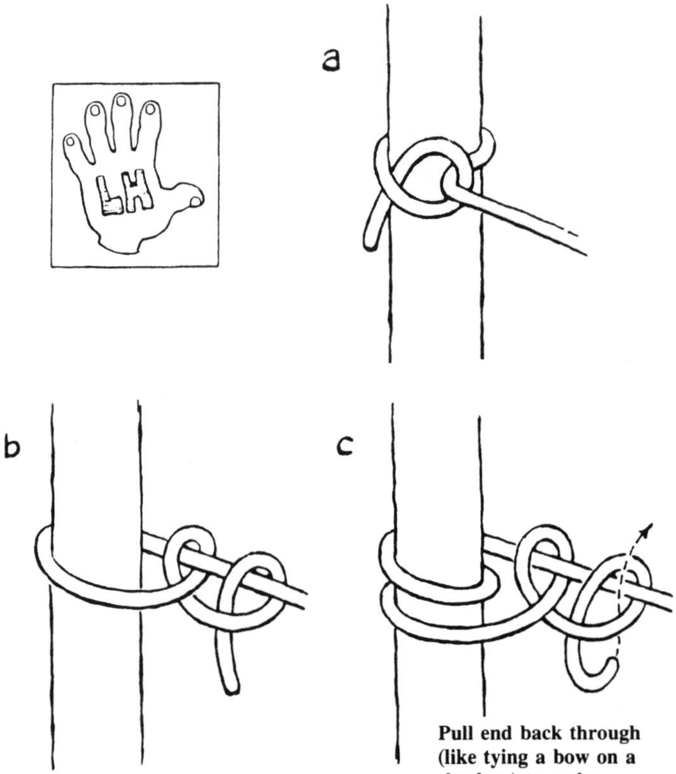
LH
a
b
c
Pull end back through (like tying a bow on a shoelace) to make the quick release feature.

***ONE HALF HITCH / TWO HALF HITCHES: Figure 2-12a, b**

Use two half-hitches to tie a rope to a tree or a boat or animal to a ring. Sailors sometimes complete a *clove hitch* with one or two half-hitches when they want infallible security. It's important that both half-hitches are alike, as illustrated, i.e. both left or right-handed. Half-hitches are one of the most essential knots in macrame.

TWO SLIPPERY HALF-HITCHES AND A ROUND TURN: Figure 2-12c

This is the quickest, most secure way to tie a boat or pack animal to a ring or bar. The "round turn" on the rail takes most of the stress off the basic knot. For faster removal, complete the hitch with a quick-release loop ("slippery" end), as illustrated.

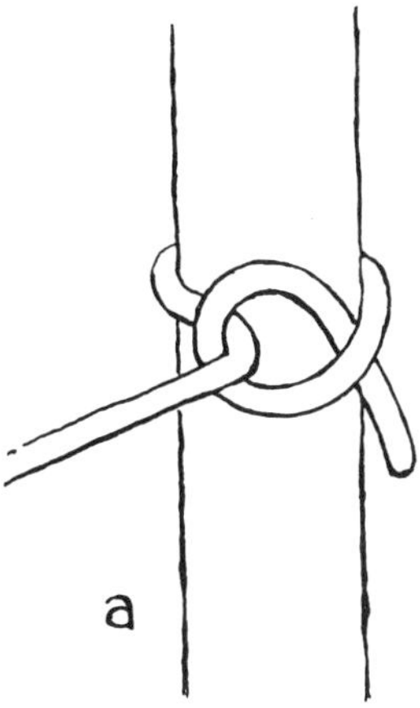
a

One half-hitch

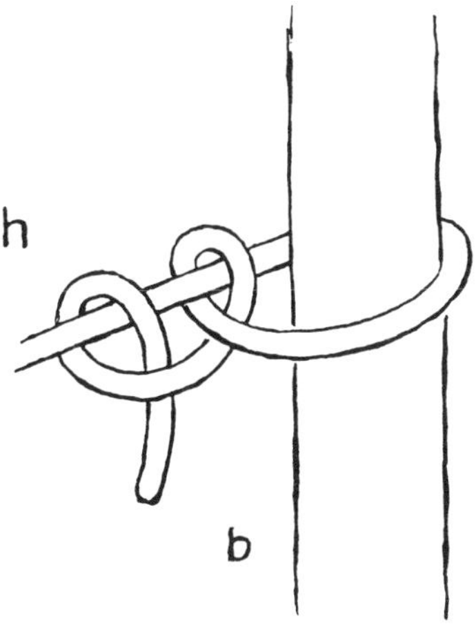
b

Two half-hitches

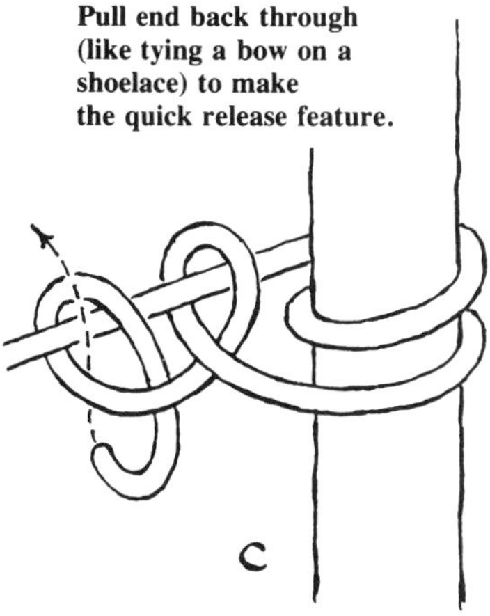
Pull end back through
(like tying a bow on a
shoelace) to make
the quick release feature.
c

Two slippery
half-hitches
and a round turn

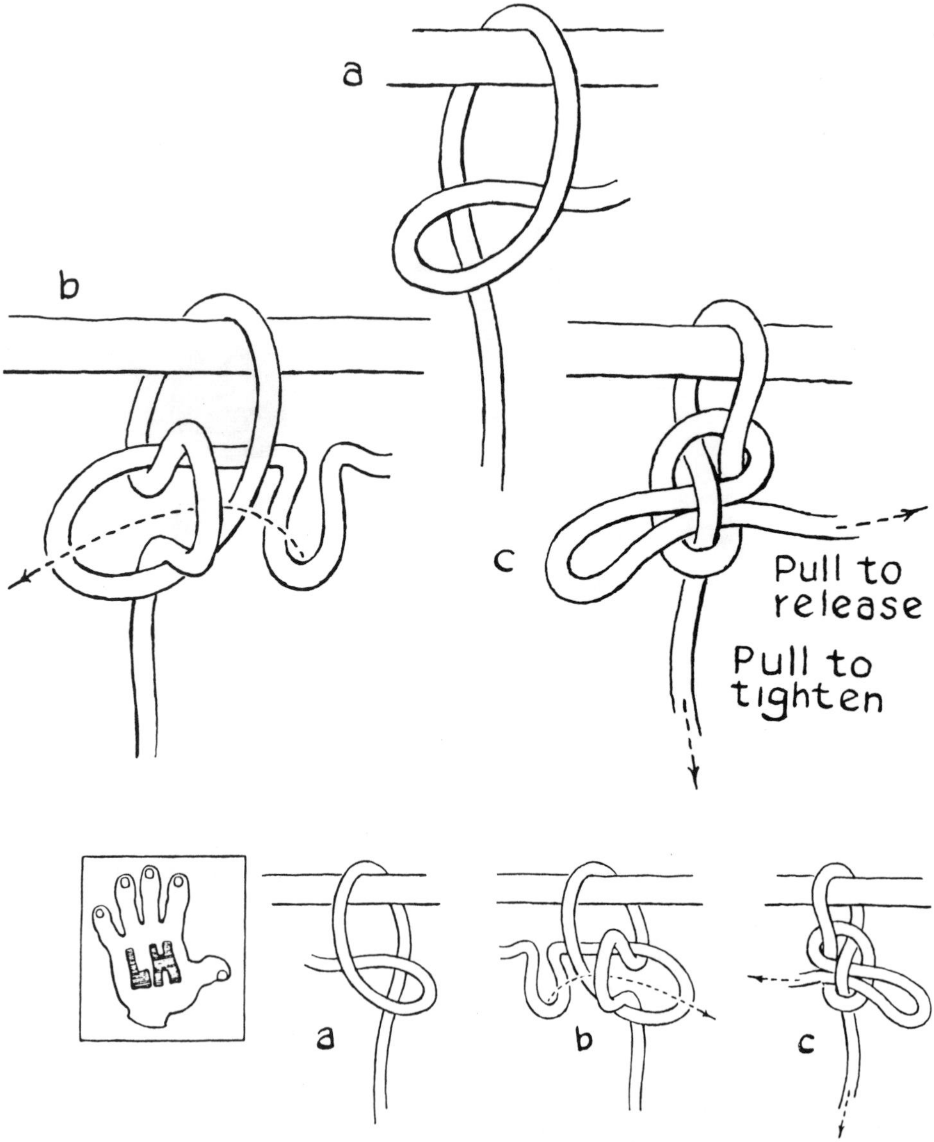

MOORING HITCH: Figure 2-13

Looks like a slippery half-hitch, but it's not. The *mooring hitch* holds fast under load yet comes apart instantly with a pull of the bitter end. You can tie it loosely and allow it to slide up to the rail like a slip knot, or jam the knot anywhere along its length so you can reach and release it without getting off your horse or out of your boat. This slick little hitch is well worth learning!

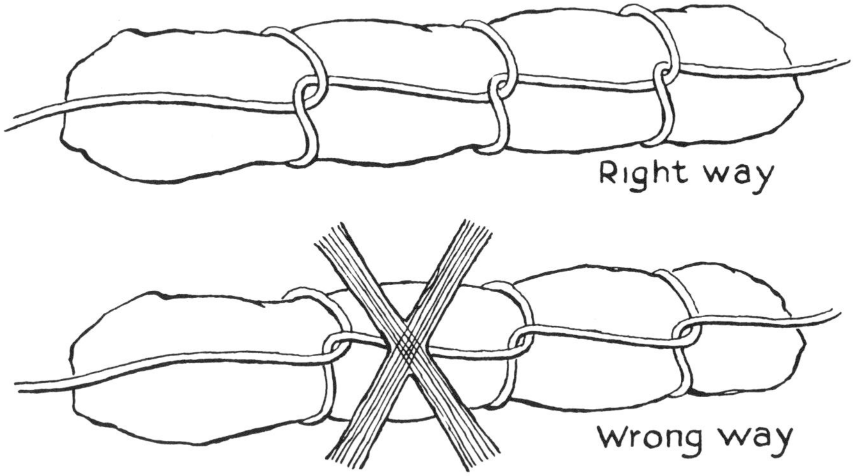

MARLINE (HAMMOCK) HITCH: Figure 2-14
(Right-hand only)

Used by sailors for centuries to secure their hammock rolls, this easy hitch is handy for tying a long bedroll, package, or roll of carpeting. Be sure the marling end goes *under* each wrapping cord as illustrated. The hitch won't hold tension if you make it backwards!

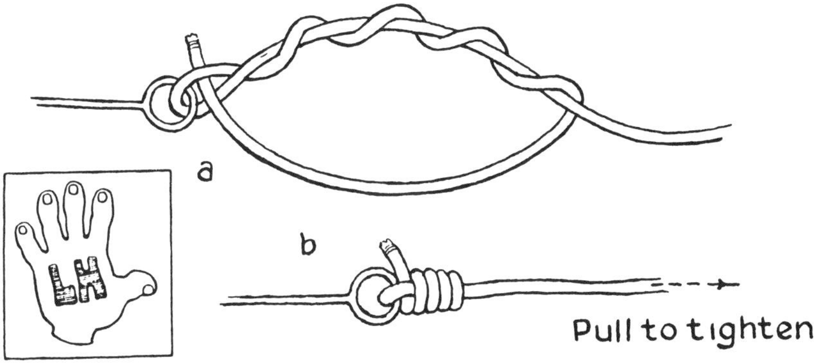

***MONOFILAMENT FISHING KNOT (CLINCH KNOT): Figure 2-15**

Popular for tying lures to monofilament fishing line, this knot holds well and is easy to make, even with cold, stiff fingers. It's about 80 percent strong. Recommended by the DuPont Company for use with nylon fishing line.

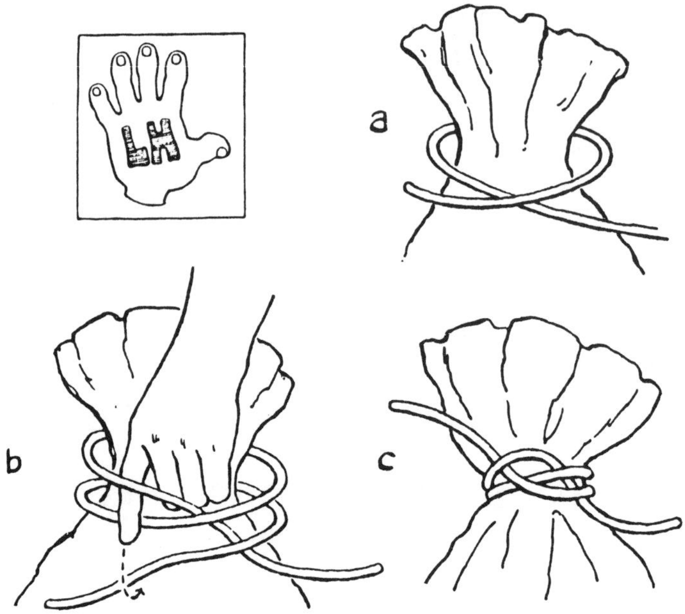

MILLER'S (CONSTRICTOR) KNOT: Figure 2-16

In the 1920's, when my best friend was a young man, he once took a job at a grain mill in Minnesota. In those days, flour sacks were tied by hand, often, with whatever knot the employees knew. On the first day of his employ, Chic doubled his required production using a *miller's knot*. Instead of earning a raise for his labor-saving efforts, my friend was transferred to another area of the mill where pay was not geared to production. Disillusioned, Chic quit the company within the week.

Similar to a clove hitch, the miller's knot is the fastest way to tie up a bulky sack. Be sure you run the first turn around the sack over the forefinger, and the rest of the turns under it. When the coil is complete, grasp the bitter end (b) of the rope with your forefinger and pull it (tight) through the top loop as illustrated. For easy removal, complete the knot with a quick- release (slippery) loop.

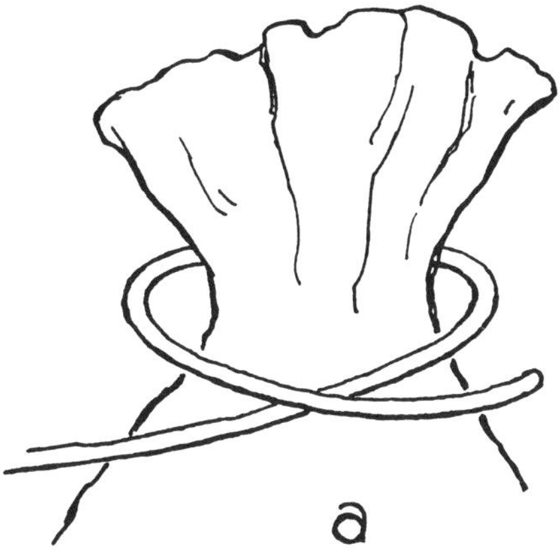

a

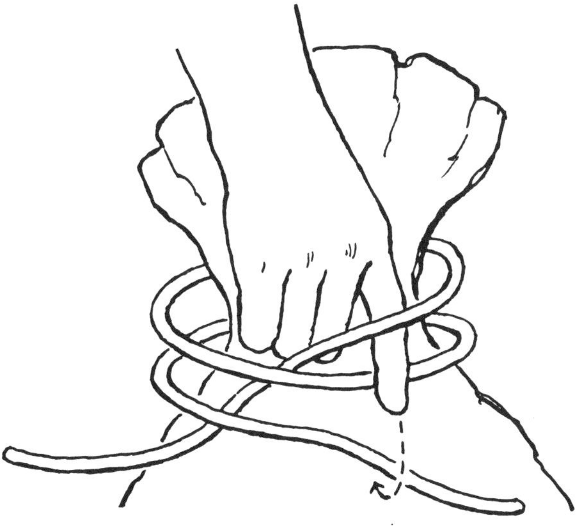

b

c

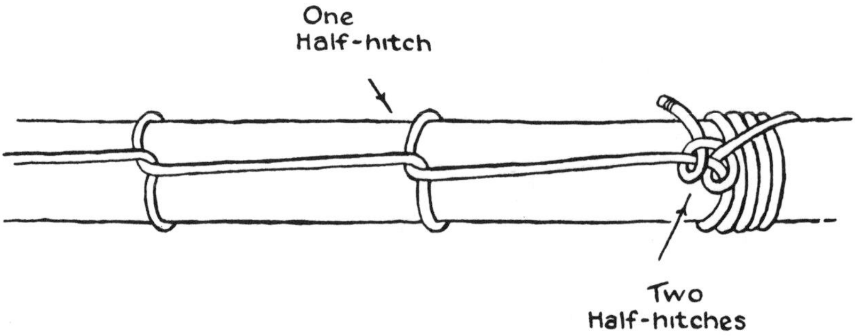

PIPE HITCH: Figure 2-17

This simple hitch is great for lifting a pipe or post vertically out of the ground. It won't slip, even on metal pipe. Simply take four or five turns around the post, cross the wrappings, and end with a pair of half-hitches. Finish off with another half-hitch high on the post (same way you complete a *timber hitch*) to keep the post vertical when pulling.

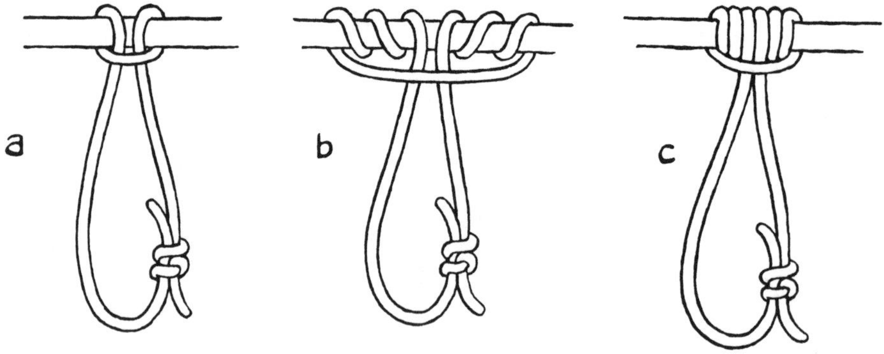

PRUSSIK KNOT: Figure 2-18 (Right-hand only)

Use the Prussik knot whenever you want an absolutely secure loop that won't slip along a tight line. Mountaineers use this knot for footholds to help them climb a vertical rope. The Prussik loop slides easily along a tight rope, yet it jams solidly when a load (horizontal or vertical) is applied. I've found this knot useful for rigging rainflies in camp and for rescuing rock-pinned canoes in a river. Make the loop from a length of parachute cord, completed with a *fisherman's knot*.

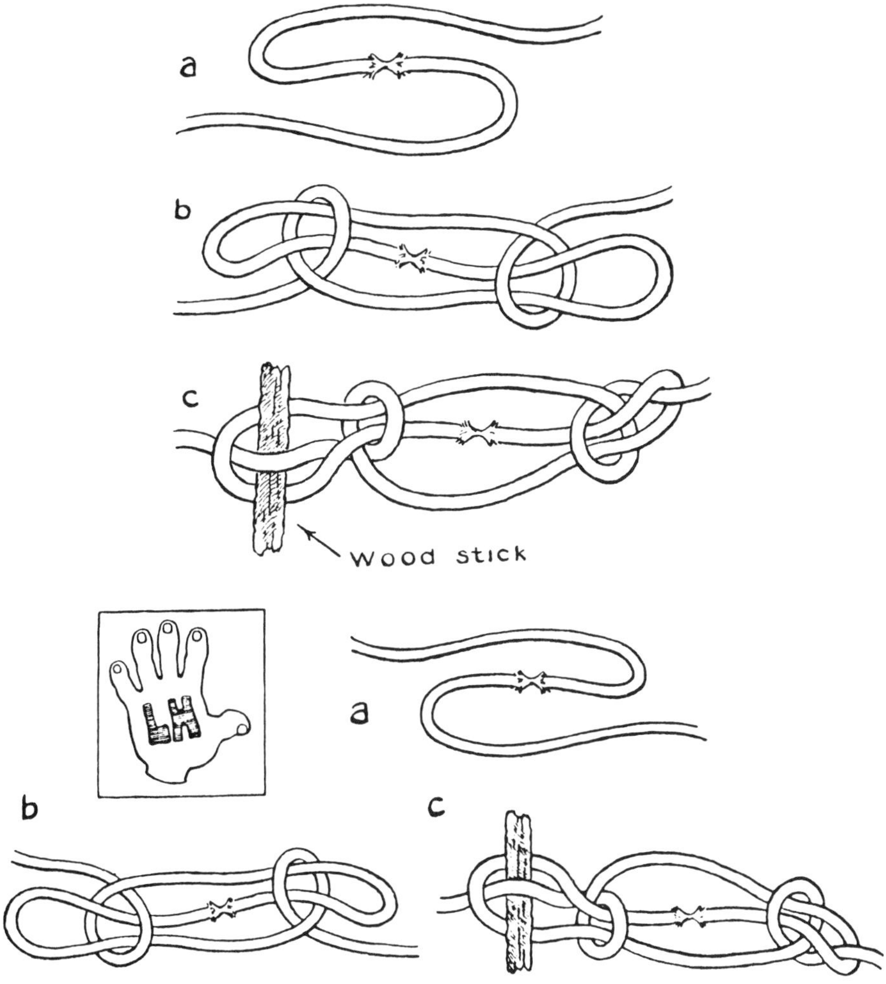

SHEEPSHANK: Figure 2-19 (Right-hand only)

Problem: your rope has a length of worn section in the middle. Eventually, you'll get around to splicing it, but for now, it will have to be used as is. The solution is the *sheepshank* — an ancient knot used by sailors to shorten rope that's too long for the job at hand.

The *sheepshank* holds only when there is tension at each end, even then, it sometimes fails. For this reason, it is best to secure it by inserting sticks of wood through the end loops as illustrated in figure 2-19.

*POWER-CINCH (TRUCKER'S KNOT): Figure 2-20

Scenario: The rutted, muddy road worsens with each yard you travel. "Gotta keep up speed, or we'll never make it," you mutter. Then, it happens: suddenly, you're axle deep in coal black ooze, and despite the determined whining of the front drive wheels, you realize you are going nowhere.

You take stock of the situation. On hand, is a shovel, 50 feet of three-eighths inch diameter nylon rope, and four sets of willing arms. With these, you'll have to free the car.

First, you shovel the "stopper" mud from under the belly of the car. Then you attach your long rope to the auto frame and rig a *power-cinch* around a smooth-barked birch nearby. Just six inches ahead is firmer ground. If you can just move the car that far.

The four man-power winch line tightens: seconds later, the car pops free, like a cookie from a mold!

The *power-cinch* is the most ingenious hitch to come along in recent years. It effectively replaces the tautline hitch and functions as a powerful pulley. Skilled canoeists use this pulley knot almost exclusively for tying canoes on cars, and it remains popular with truckers for securing heavy loads in place. Use it any time you need to tie an object tightly onto a cartop or truck bed.

Begin the hitch by forming the overhand loop shown in Figure 2-20, step 1. Pull the loop through as in step 2. It is important that you make the loop *exactly* as shown. It will look okay if you make it backwards, but it won't work!

If you're tying something onto a car top, run the bitter (free) end of the hitch through an S-hook attached to the bumper. (Step 4.) Snug the hitch and secure it with a pair of half-hitches around the bight, as illustrated in step 5. Or, for ease of removal, end the power-cinch with a quick-release half-hitch, as in step 6..

The power-cinch as a multiple pulley: For additional power, as in the above scenario, form a second loop in the *free end* of the rope as shown in step 7. This will double the mechanical advantage, albeit increase friction. This rescue technique — commonly set up with aluminum carabiners instead of rope loops — was popularized by the Nantahala Outdoor Center (a whitewater canoe and kayak school) as the "Z-drag," because the rope pattern forms a lazy Z when viewed from overhead.

The basic *power-cinch* however, is probably all you'll ever need. I consider it the most useful hitch there is.

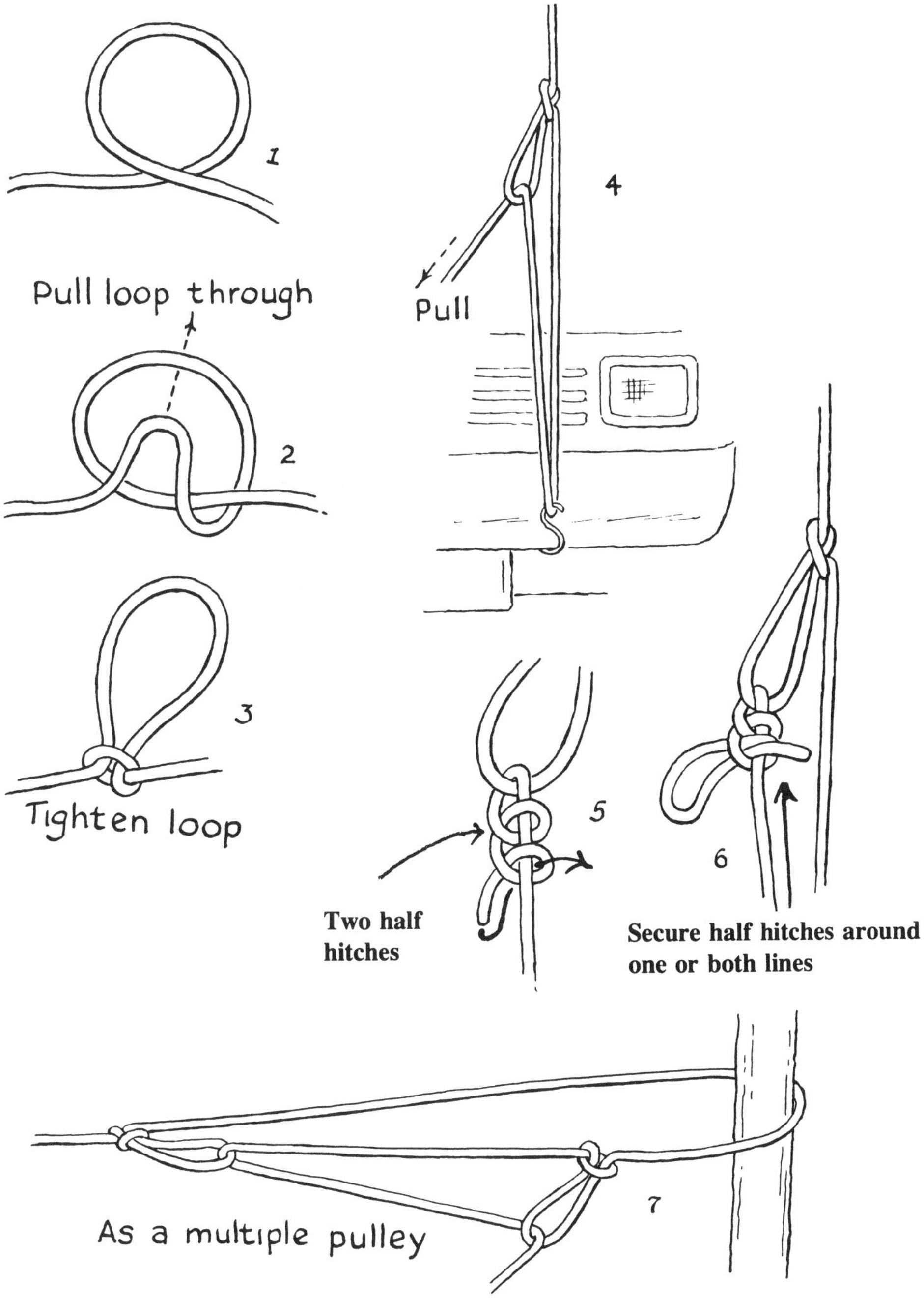

IF ONLY I HAD USED A QUICK-RELEASE KNOT!

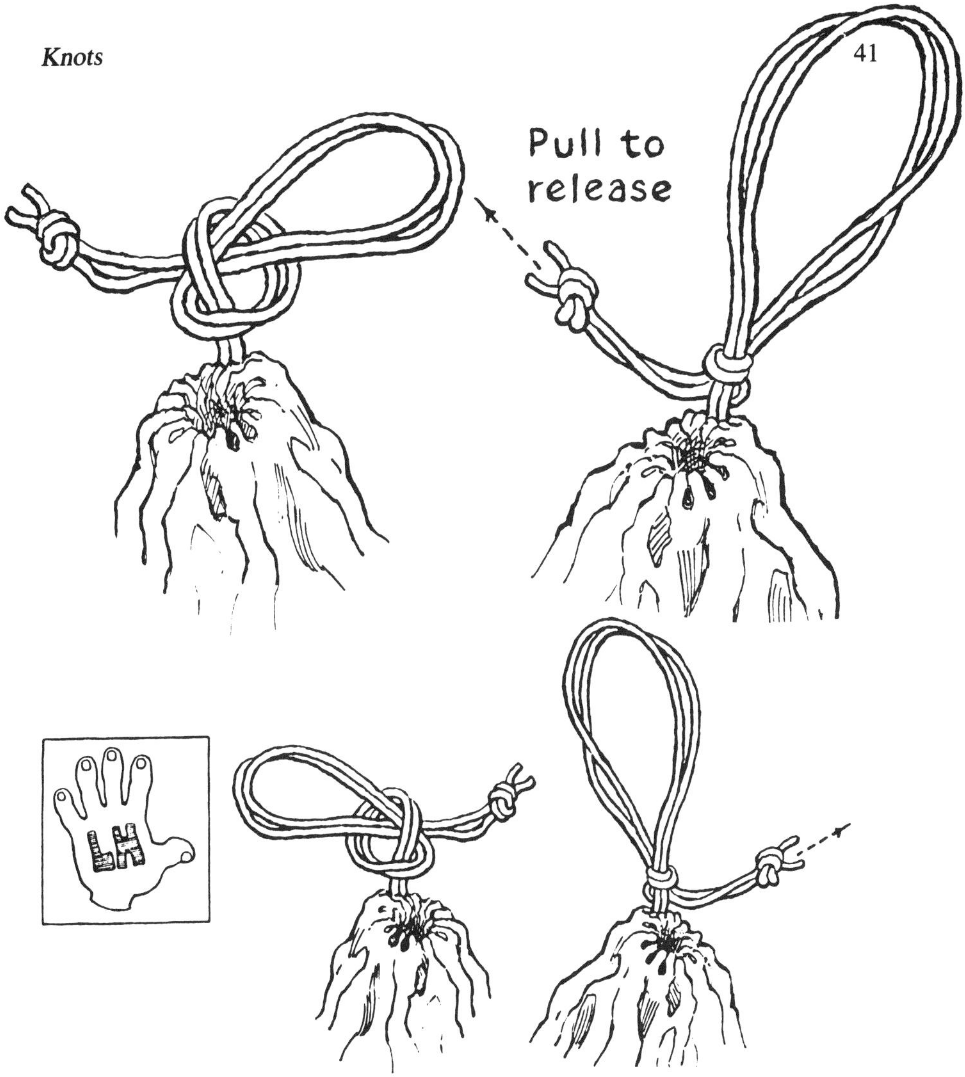

*QUICK-RELEASE (SLIPPERY) LOOP: Figure 2-21

Nothing is more frustrating than untying a bunch of tight knots when you're breaking camp in the morning. If you end your knots with a "quick-release" (slippery) loop, as illustrated, you'll be able to untie your ties with a single pull. Form the "QR" feature by running the bitter end of the rope back through the completed knot — same as making a "bow" when you tie your shoes.

Use a simple overhand knot with a slippery loop to seal drawstring bags and stuff sacks. The plastic "cord-locks" sold in camping stores for this purpose are for people who don't know how to tie slippery knots.

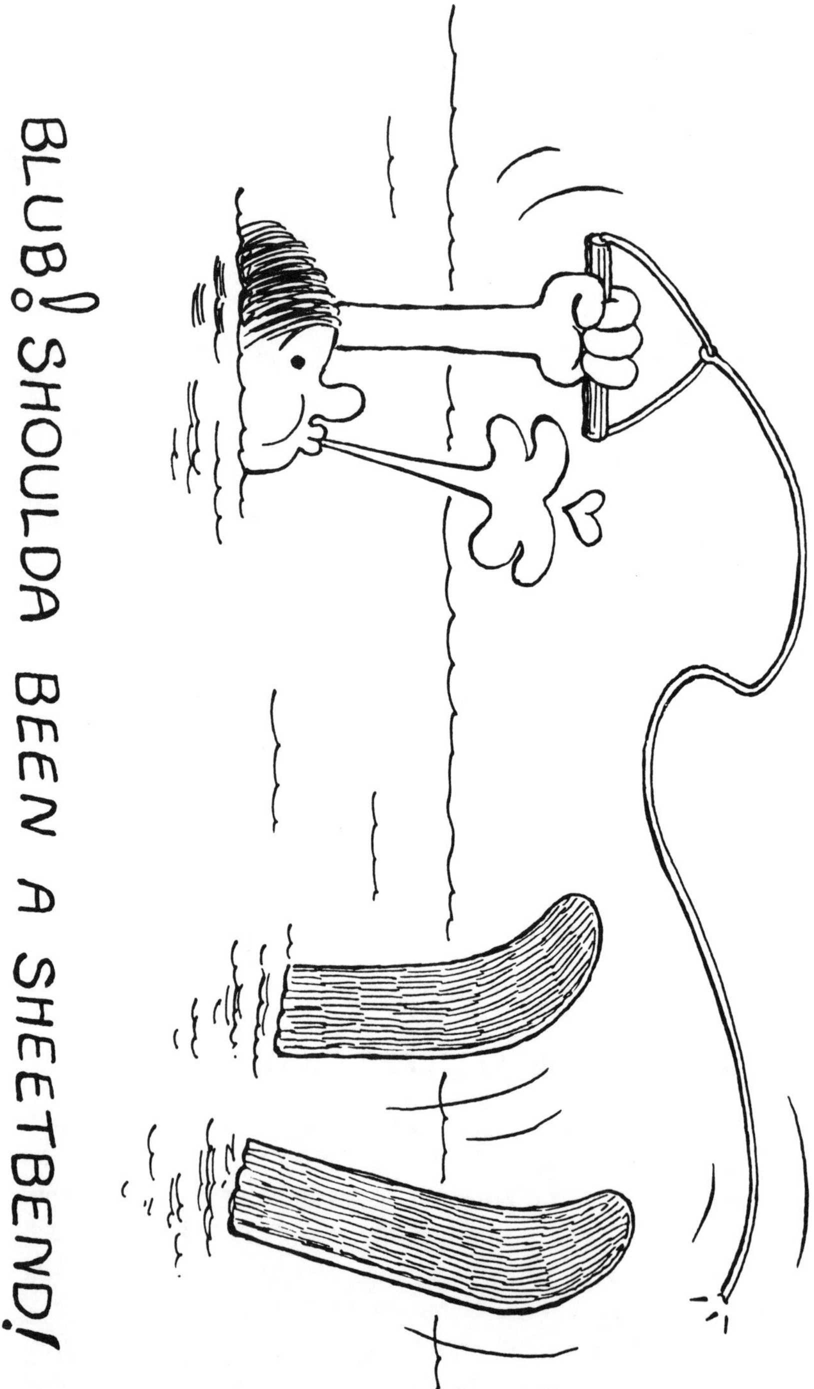
BLUB! SHOULDA BEEN A SHEETBEND!

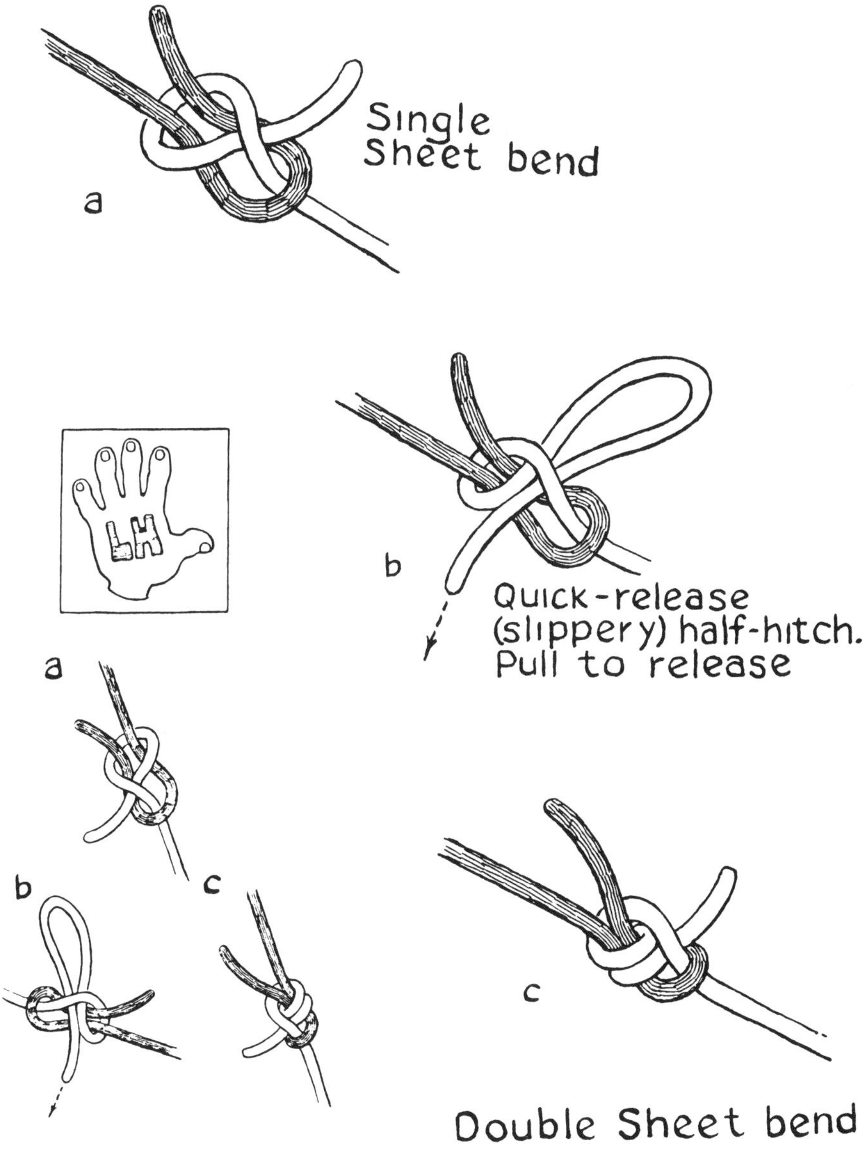

***SHEET-BEND/DOUBLE SHEET-BEND/
SLIPPERY SHEET-BEND: Figure 2-22a,b,c**

The *sheet-bend* is one of the most useful knots, and one of the few that can be used for tying two ropes together, even when rope sizes and materials differ greatly. Some years ago, a friend of mine won five dollars when he fixed a broken water-ski tow-rope with this bend. When the tow-line snapped, the ski-boat captain bet my friend that he couldn't tie the two ends of the slick polypropylene rope back together tightly enough to hold. My friend won the bet and skied the remainder of the day on the repaired line.

It's important that the bitter (free) ends of the sheet-bend be on the *same side*, as illustrated, otherwise the knot will be unreliable. If you want the knot to release instantly, end it with a quick-release (slippery) half hitch (figure 22b).

For greater security, especially in plastic rope, use the *double sheet-bend* (Becket Bend). Same as the single version but with an extra coil around the standing loop (figure 22c).

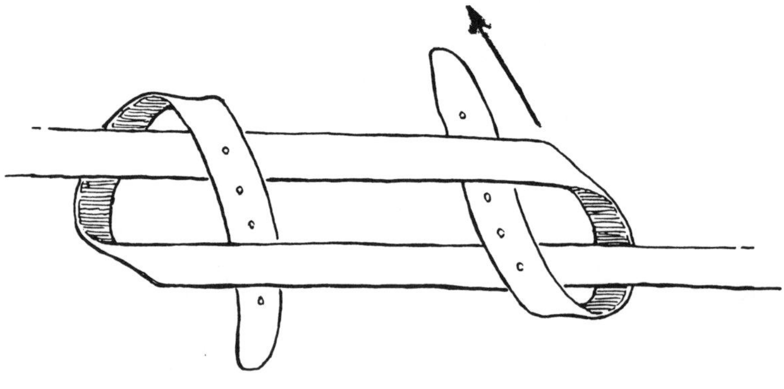

STRAP KNOT: Figure 2-23

Not a knot, per se, but a handy method of tying leather or nylon straps together to form a long rope. Nothing more than a single half-hitch, each made opposite to the other.

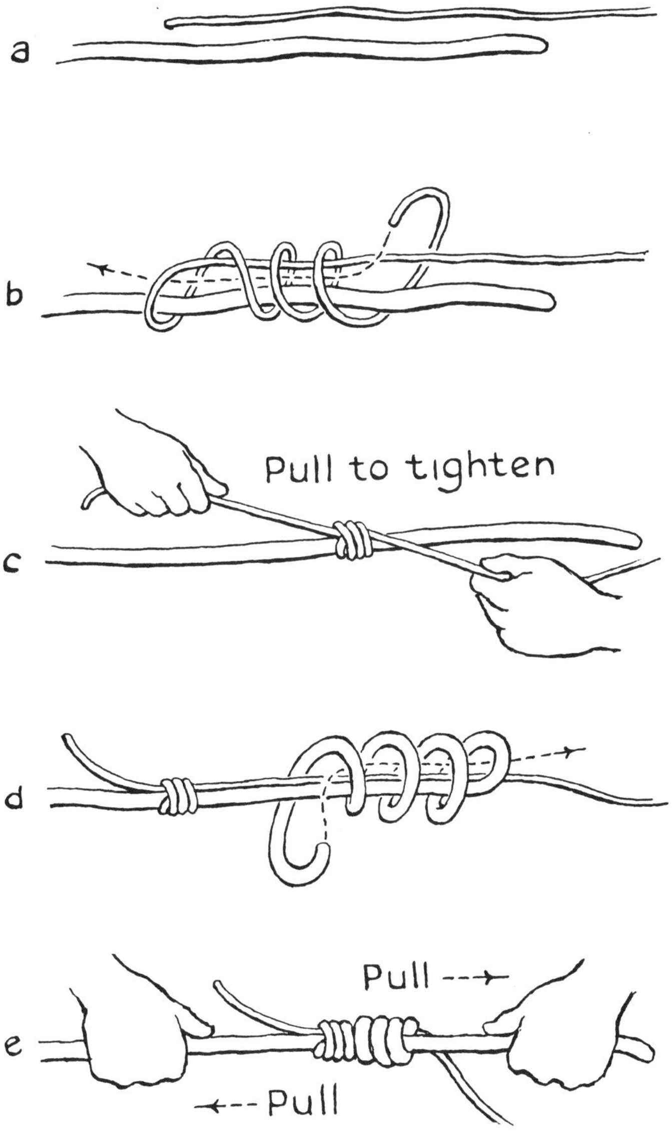

S-KNOT: Figure 2-24

Here's an artistic way to tie two ropes together. Similar to a *fisherman's knot*, the *S-knot* has more coils and so is probably more secure, especially in slippery ropes.

Place the ends of the rope parallel to one another and take three or more complete turns around the two ropes, then run the bitter (free) end down the center of the knot. Do the same with the other rope. Finally, slide the knots together to complete the *S-knot*.

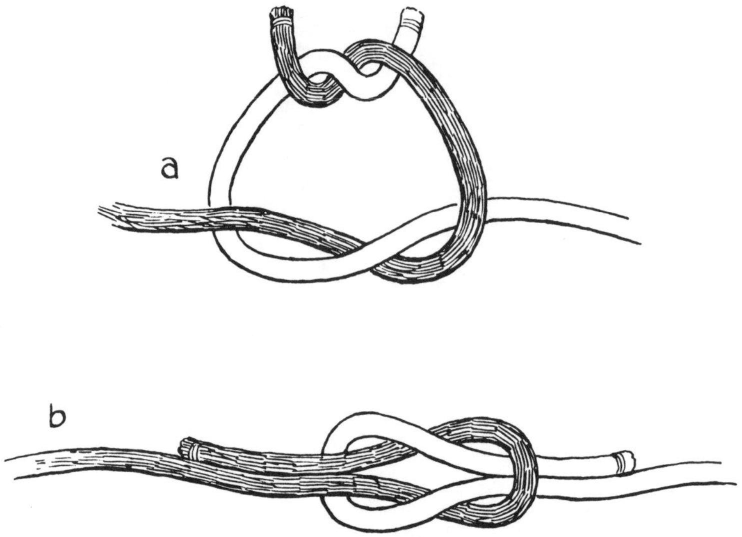

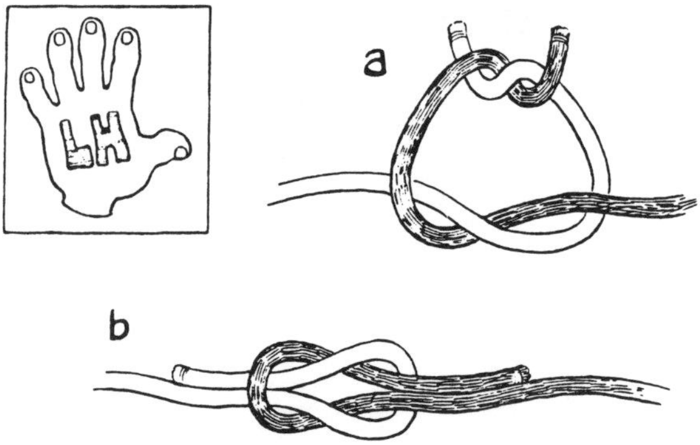

SQUARE KNOT (REEF KNOT): Figure 2-25

For centuries sailors have used this knot for reefing sails and tying things aboard ship. The *square knot* is still used for this purpose but is probably more popular for tying packages, gauze dressings, tourniquets, and other medical applications. *Don't* use this knot for joining two ropes together if they will be under load! The *square-knot* jams under tension and falls apart (it becomes two half-hitches) if the ropes are very dissimilar or the pull comes unevenly. Use a *sheet-bend*, fisherman's knot, or two *bowlines* for joining ropes.

To form a *square knot* rather than a common granny, complete each over-hand knot *opposite* the other. Thus, if the first knot is formed right-handed (right over left), the second must be made left-handed (left over right).

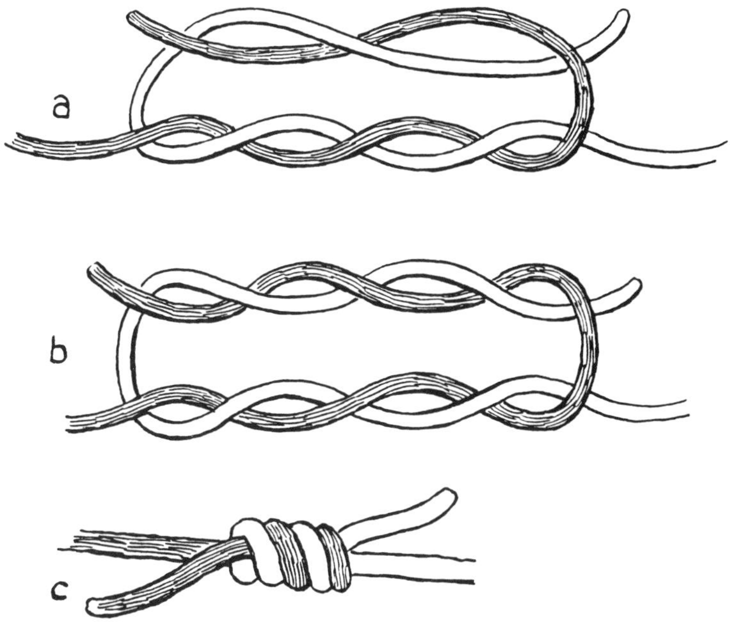

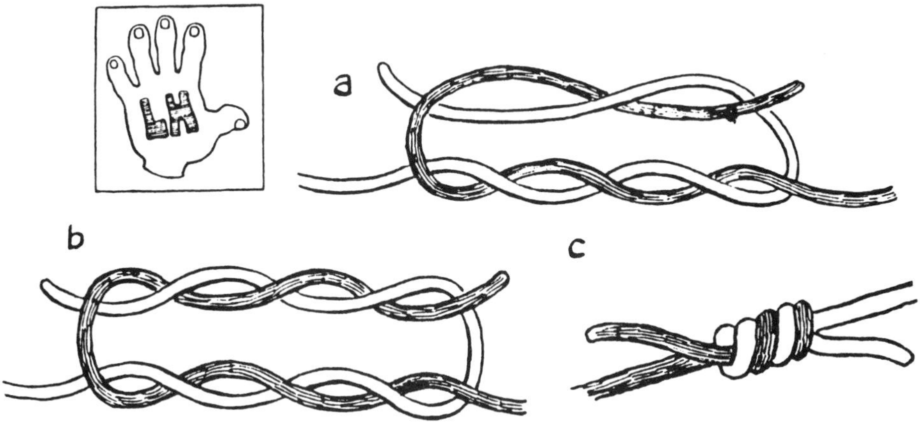

SURGEON'S KNOT: Figure 2-26a,b

Simply a square knot with an extra turn on the bottom, and perhaps an additional turn on top (there are two forms of the knot as illustrated). The *surgeon's knot* is much more secure in slippery materials than the traditional square knot. Whitewater kayakers use a slippery (with quick-release loop) *surgeon's knot* to tie the slick nylon waist ties of their life jackets.

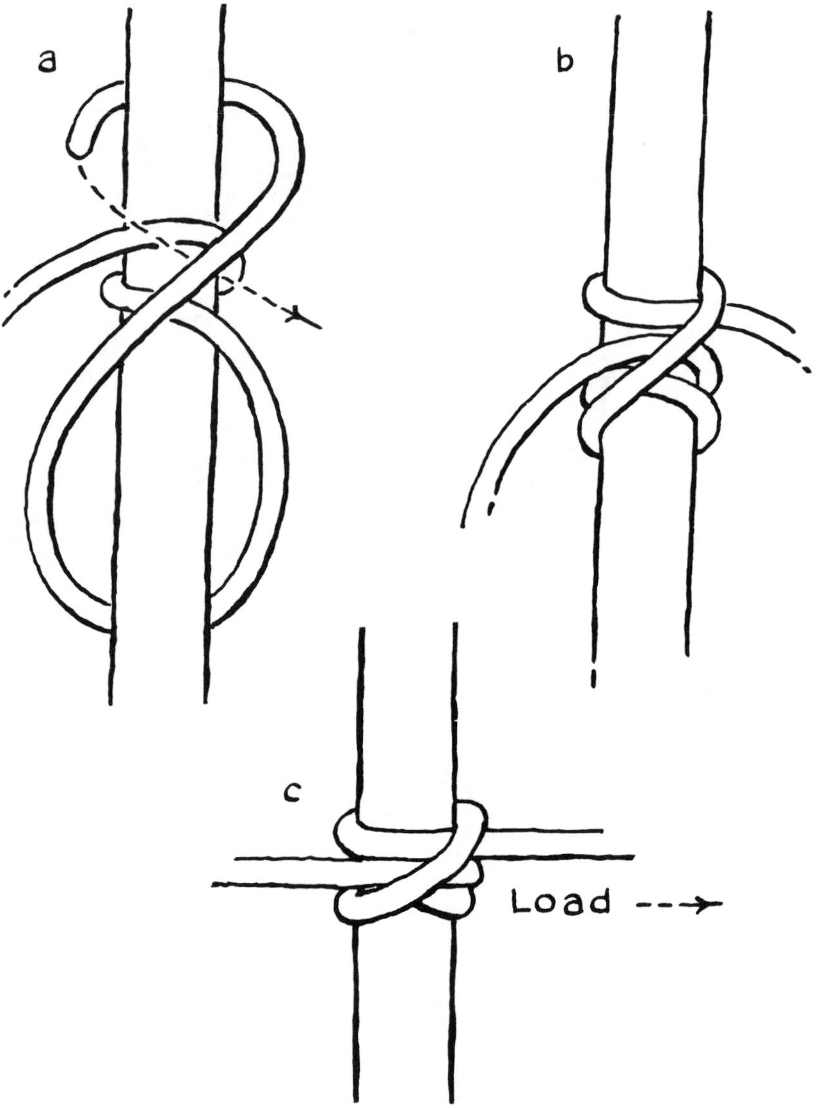
a
b
c
Load

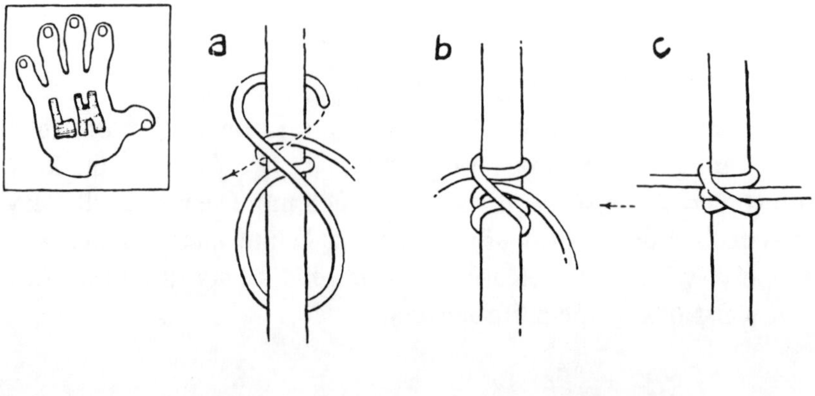
LH
a
b
c

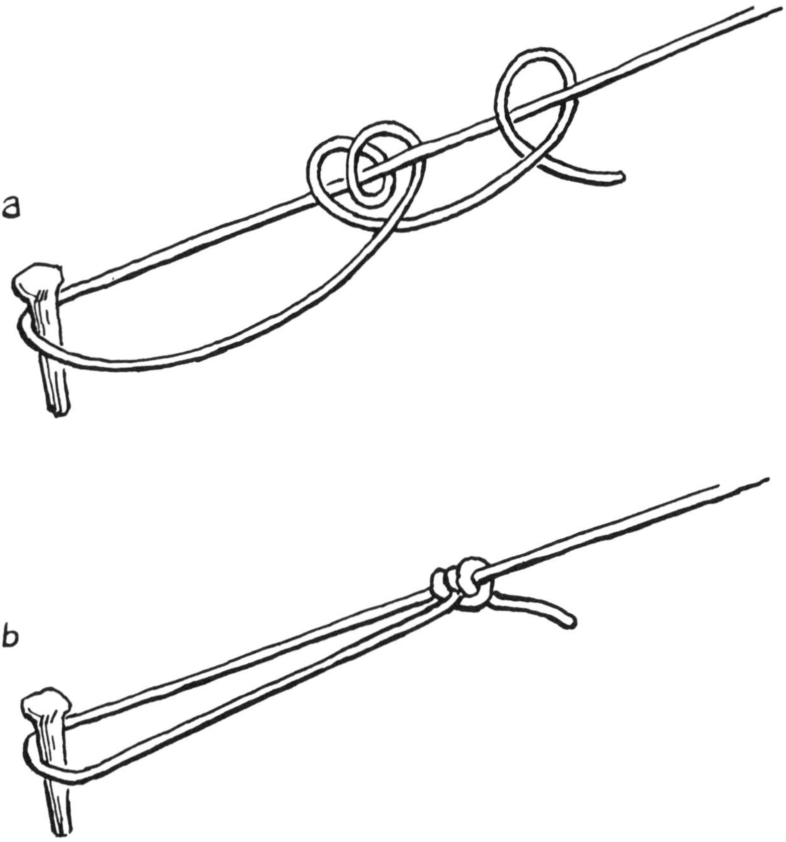

a

b

TAUT-LINE (ROLLING HITCH): Figure 2-27a,b

Sailors use the *rolling hitch* whenever they want to attach a rope to a spar. The knot is much more secure than a *clove hitch*, especially when the load is parallel to the spar.

The same hitch can be applied to a tight rope that's secured around a tree or tent stake, in which case it is called the "taut-line hitch" (figure 2-27b). Boy Scouts prefer the *taut- line hitch* for anchoring their tent guy lines. The hitch slides freely, yet jams under load.

The original *rolling hitch* (figure 2-27a) is a fine knot for its intended purpose. The *taut-line* version, however, is less versatile and much inferior to the more powerful *power-cinch (trucker's knot)* explained on page 38.

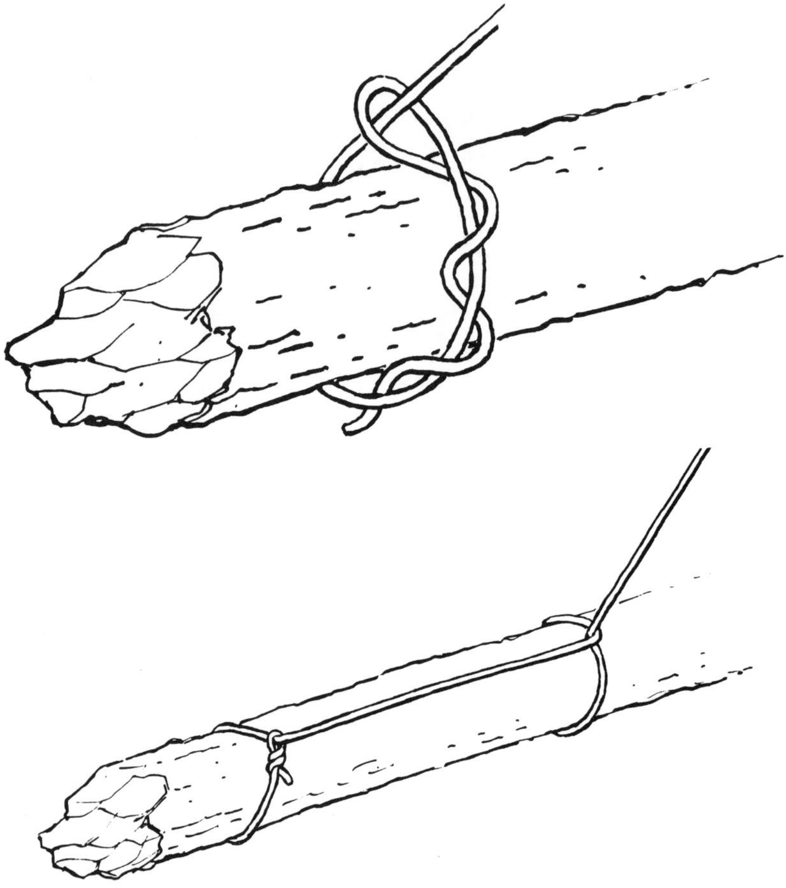

***TIMBER HITCH: Figure 2-28 (Right-hand only)**

Use the *timber hitch* for hauling logs, timbers, heavy pipe, and cumbersome objects. It's very strong (about 70 percent), won't slip, and it can't jam, no matter how heavy the load. I often attach the tow rope to my Jeep with a timber hitch when clearing brush and trees. It always comes apart easily. It's best to complete the *timber hitch* with a half-hitch near the hauling end to keep a long log from twisting.

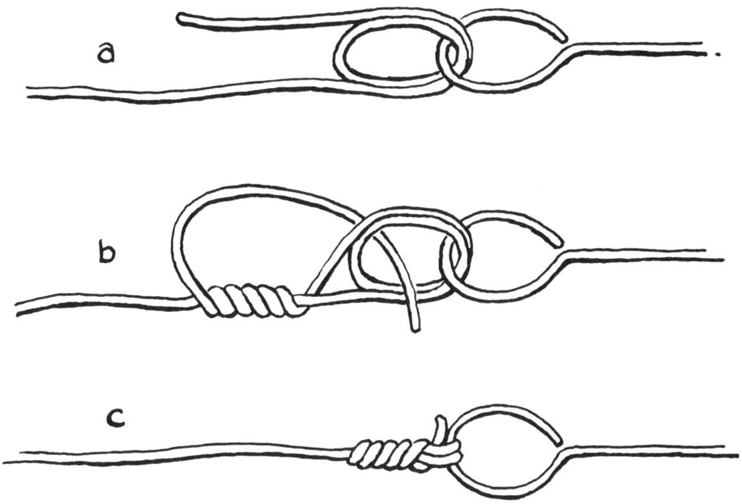

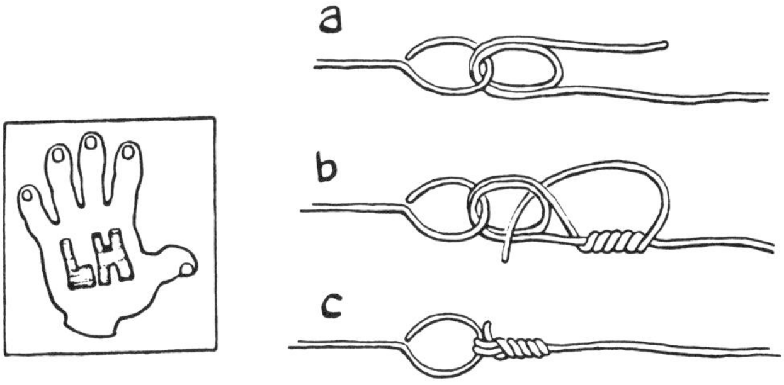

TRILENE (FISHING) knot: Figure 2-29

Berkley researchers recommend this knot for tying lures in slippery monofilament line. The *Trilene knot* is a cross between an *anchor bend* and a *clinch knot*. Berkley tests reveal that the knot yields 80-90 percent of the line's breaking strength. Tip: wet the knot before tightening it; this will lubricate the line and reduce damage caused by the heat-of- friction.

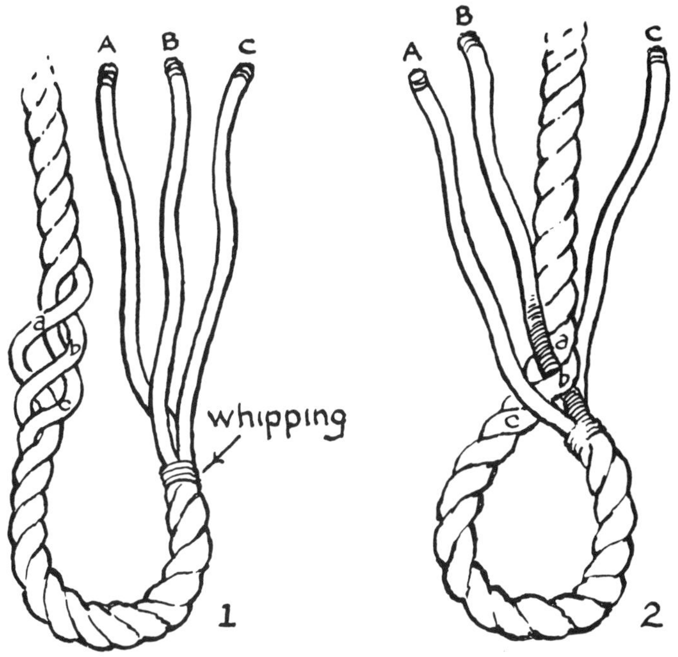

EYE SPLICE: Figure 2-30

You can form a loop at the end of a line with a bowline, but it's not nearly as strong as an eye splice. And when it comes to beauty, there's no contest between a bulky knot and a symmetrical splice.

Procedure: (1) Whip the rope (optional) about six inches from the end and unravel the strands which have been identified as A, B, C. (2) Form a loop (eye) and begin the splice, weaving the strands through a, b, c, as illustrated. Note that each strand is tucked through the rope from right to left, *against* the lay. Twist the strands *clockwise* as you pull them through the rope, and maintain the same tension on each strand. This will give the splice a smooth, untwisted look. Splicing will go easier if you have a pointed tool (fid) to open the lay. (4) Reverse the splice and tuck C under c. (5) Reverse splice again and continue to weave the strands as shown.

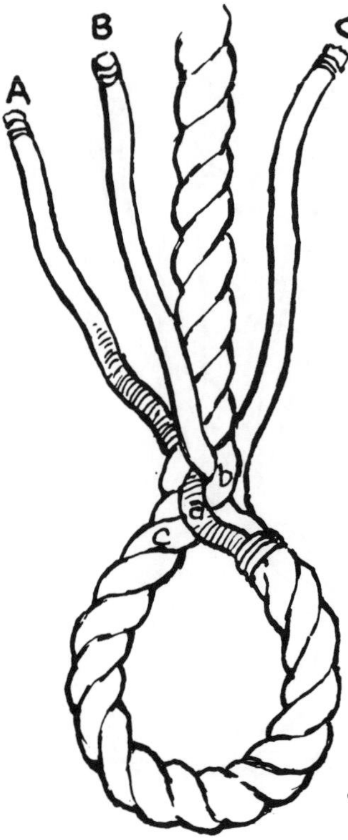

3

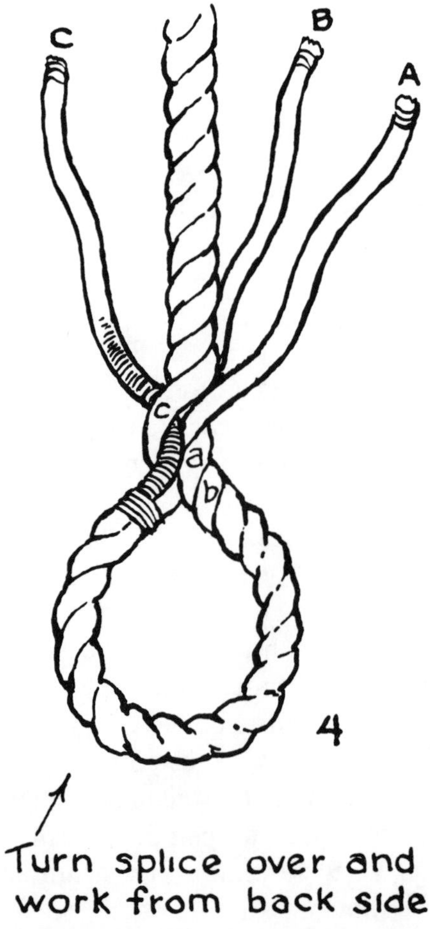

4

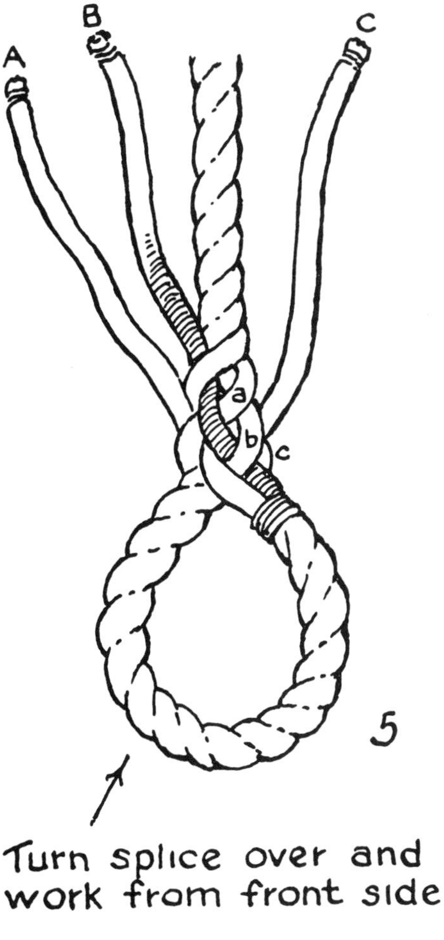

5

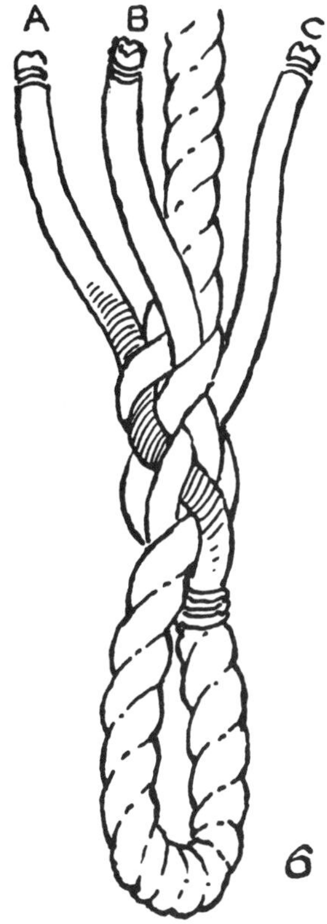

6

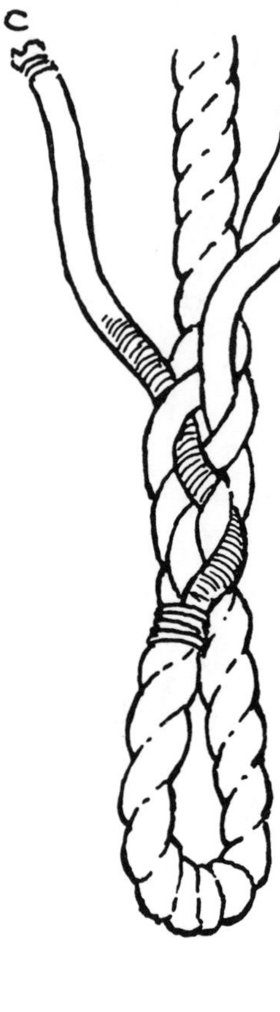

7

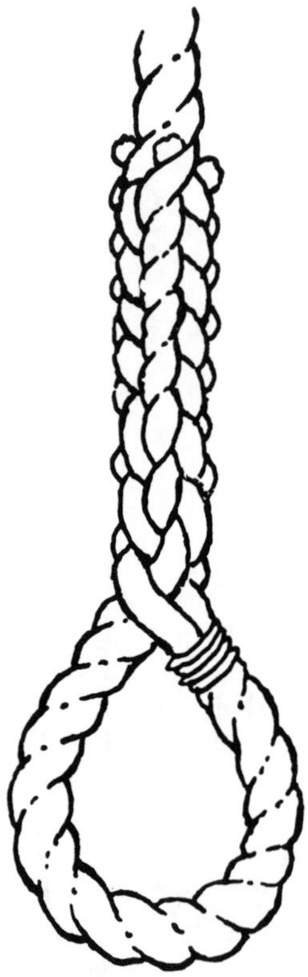

8

You may continue to splice until the strands are all buried (maximum strength is reached with three tucks), or snip off each strand a tuck or two apart to taper the finished splice (more artistic). Finish by rolling the splice firmly between your hands. Flame-whip the ends of the protruding strands (synthetic line) and roll again. Cut off the temporary whipping and your splice is complete.

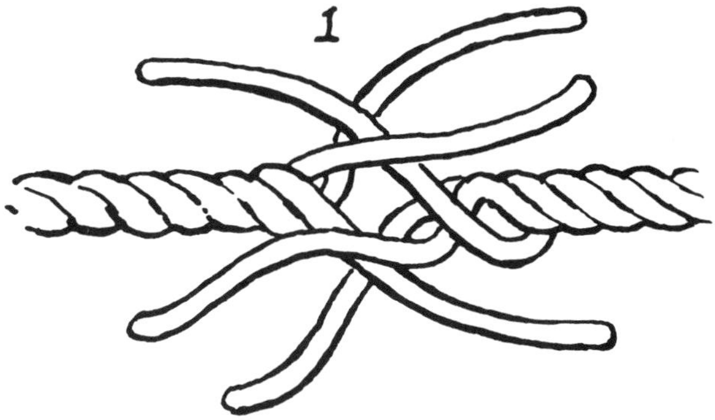

SHORT SPLICE: Figure 2-31

This is the strongest (reduces the line's breaking strength by about ten percent) way to join two ropes.

Procedure: (1) Untwist the strands of each rope a half dozen turns, then, "marry" alternating strands together. (2) To keep the "non-working" strands temporarily out of the way, you may want to lightly whip or tape them to the rope body. Some sailors also tape the ends of each strand to keep them from unraveling.

The rest of the splice is academic: simply tuck each strand alternately *against the lay* of the rope, as illustrated. Three or four tucks ensures maximum strength, but you can make the splice as long as you like. Finish by rolling the completed splice briskly between your hands, then flame-singe (synthetic rope) the exposed strand ends. A final roll between your hands or underfoot, rounds up the splice.

2

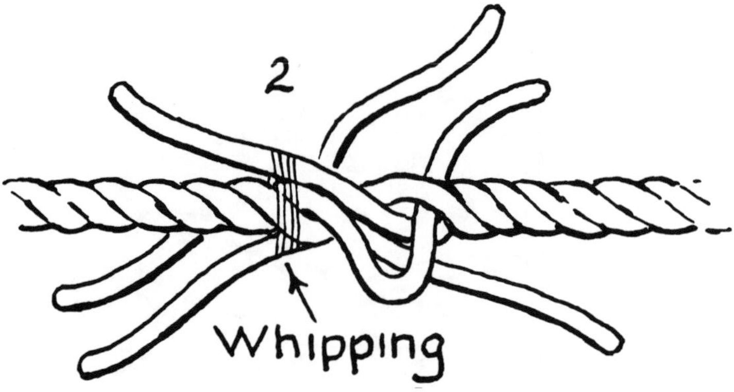

3

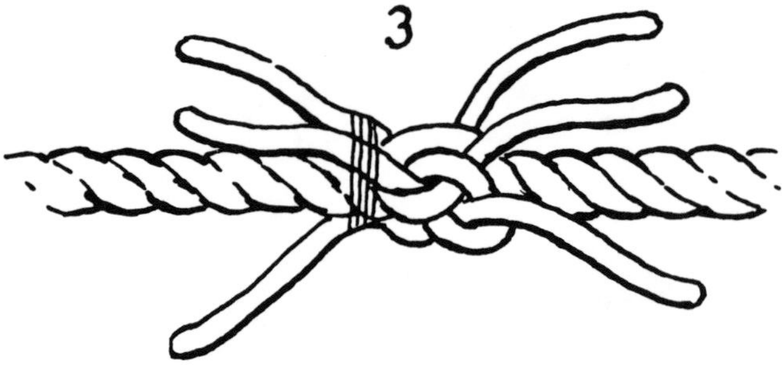

4

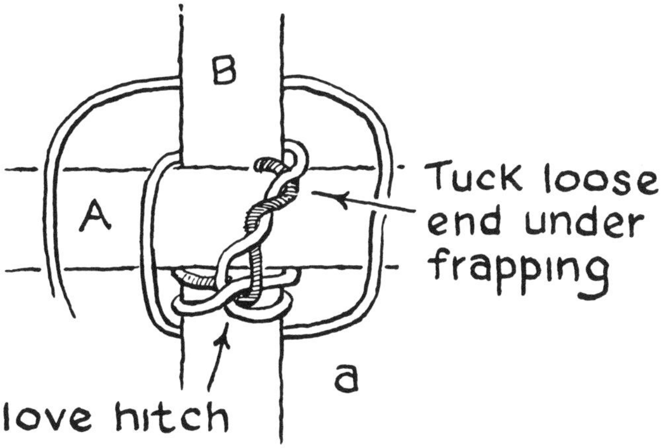

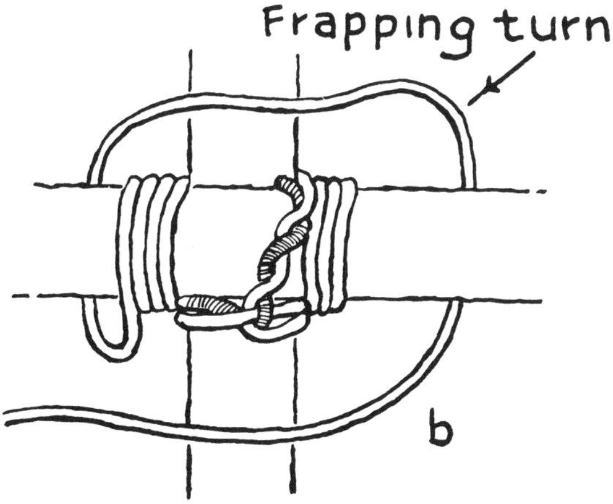

SQUARE LASHING: Figure 2-32

Use this classic lashing to secure two spars that touch each other at the point where they cross. Begin the lashing with a *clove hitch* or *timber hitch* around the vertical spar, just below the cross-piece (A). Run the cord over the horizontal bar, around behind the vertical bar, then back over the face of the horizontal bar on the left. Tighten snugly, then bring the cord behind the vertical bar and up the right front side of the horizontal bar. Repeat this three or four times. Finish with two "frapping" (binding) turns to tighten the lashing, and lock everything in place with a clove hitch on the crosspiece.

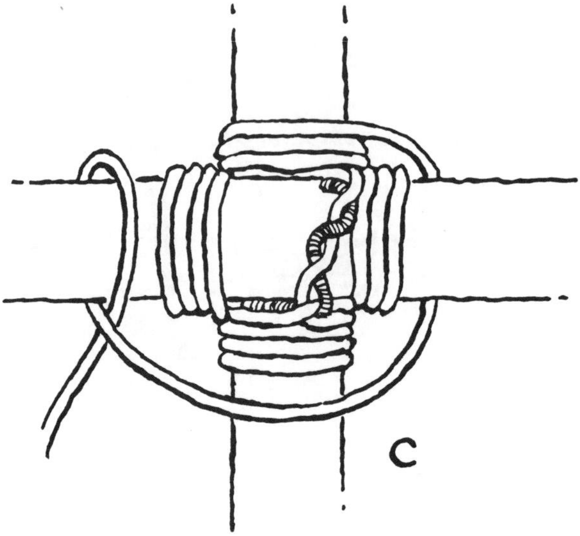

c

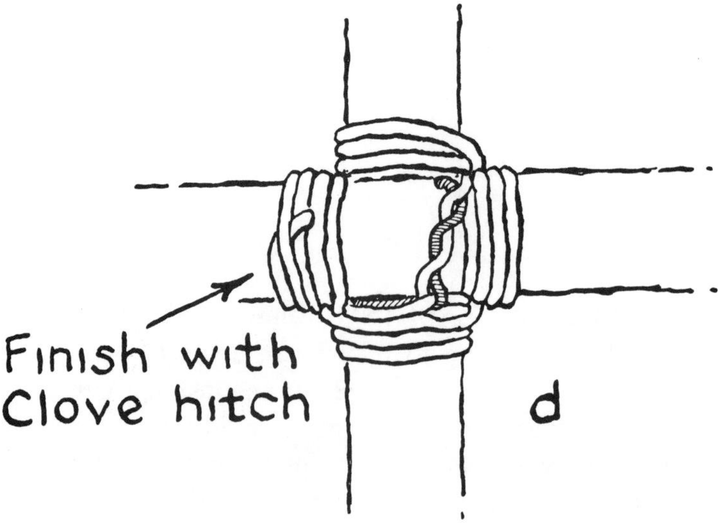

d

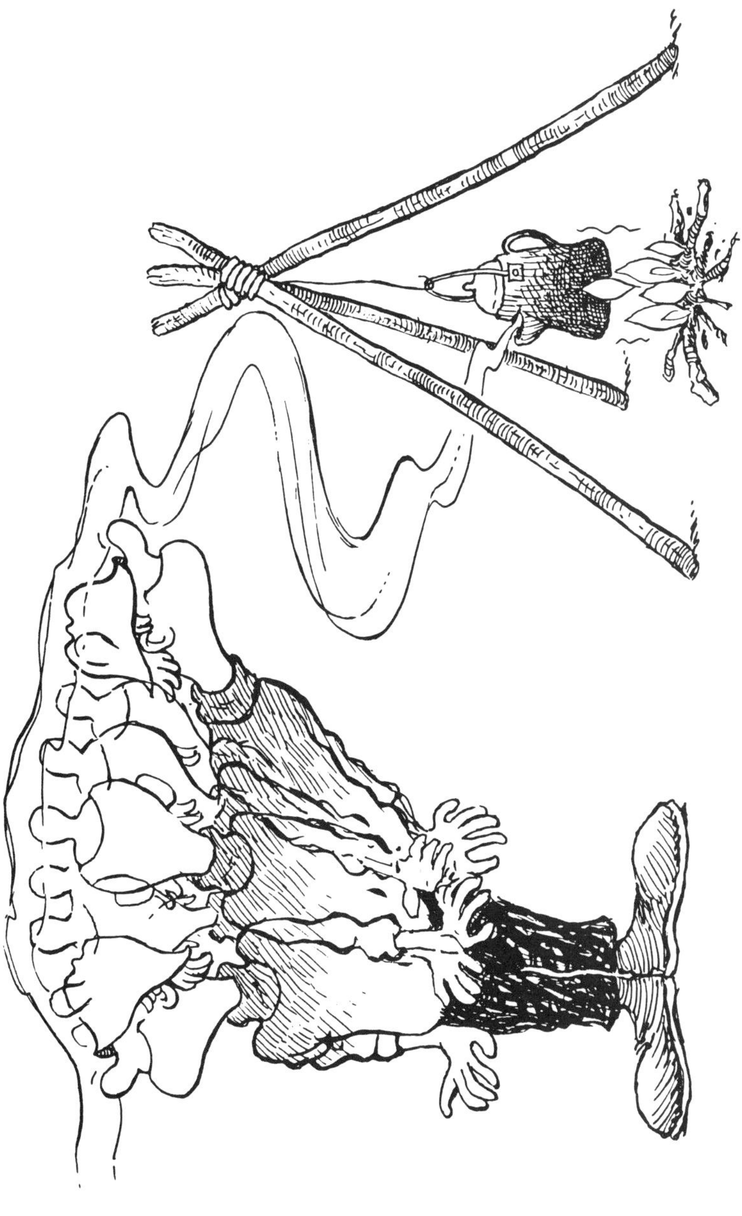

TRIPOD LASHING: Figure 32

Here's a fast, secure way to make a support for a camera or coffee pot. If you end the lashing with a quick-release (slippery) *clove hitch*, it will come undone instantly.

Procedure: Lay out the spars on the ground with the center spar pointing away from the other two. Begin with a *clove hitch* or *timber hitch* at the end of one of the side spars. Then, make six to eight loose turns around all three spars and finish up with two frapping (binding) turns between each spar. A *clove hitch* on the center bar completes the lashing. Note: the *sheer lashing* (not illustrated) — which is used to secure parallel spars in bridges and tables — is simply a two-legged version of the *tripod lashing*.

a

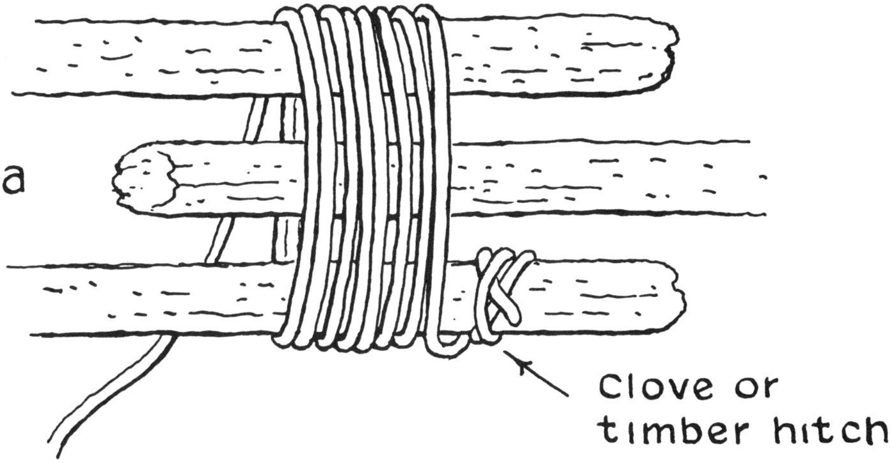

b

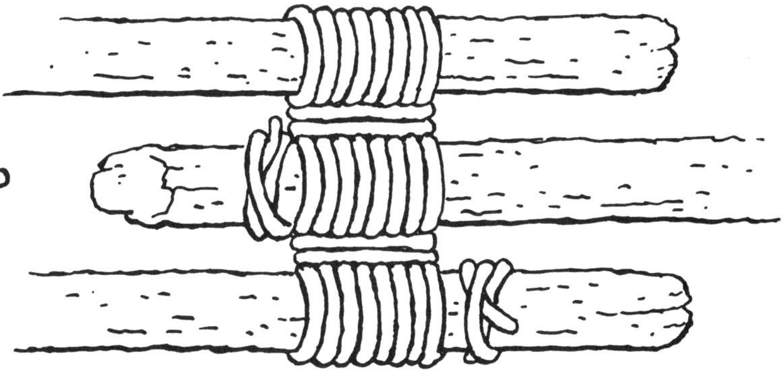

INDEX